POWER TO PRAY

God's Immense Purposes for Our Simple Prayers

DON ANDRESON

Power To Pray
Copyright © 2022 by Don Andreson

All rights reserved. No part of this publication may be reproduced, distributed, or transmitted in any form or by any means, including photocopying, recording, or other electronic or mechanical methods, without the prior written permission of the author, except in the case of brief quotations embodied in critical reviews and certain other non-commercial uses permitted by copyright law.

ISBN
978-1-957378-29-9 (Paperback)
978-1-957378-28-2 (eBook)

Thanks Nancy – my greatest lover, my greatest partner, my greatest friend. Without you, this book would not be…And your prayers have changed the world in a thousand ways.

TABLE OF CONTENTS

Acknowledgment 1

Introduction 3

Chapter 1   Our Name is House of Prayer 5

Chapter 2   When Shall I Pray? 21

Chapter 3   Prayer is Work 33

Chapter 4   Why Prayer? 43

Chapter 5   Where Should We Pray? 51

Chapter 6   Our Prayer and The Helper 61

Chapter 7   The Rule of Wrestling 75

Chapter 8   The Throne and The Lamb 95

Chapter 9   Authority to Pray for Nations 107

Chapter 10 Or Are We Just Kidding Ourselves? 123

Chapter 11 Praying That Works 145

Final Vision: United To Jesus 157

Study / Discussion Guide

Chapter 1 Our Name is House of Prayer 165

Chapter 2 When Shall I Pray? 169

Chapter 3 Prayer is Work! 174

Chapter 4 Why Prayer? 179

Chapter 5 Where Should We Pray? 183

Chapter 6 Our Prayer and the Helper 186

Chapter 7 The Rule of Wrestling 191

Chapter 8 The Throne and The Lamb 198

Chapter 9 Authority to Pray for Nations 206

Chapter 10 Or Are We Just Kidding Ourselves? 210

Chapter 11 Praying That Works 215

Bibliography 219
About the Author 221

ACKNOWLEDGMENT

There are so many people who have discipled and challenged me to learn to pray that I cannot possibly list them all. Some are well known. Some have written books. Some are little-known and will never write. Certainly the list includes Dr. Harold John Ockerga–my "growing up" pastor at Park Street Church in Boston. It also includes Dwight Ham discipling pastor many years further on. Through him I was introduced to Derek Prince, Mahesh Chavda, James Goll, Mike Bickel, and Jim Croft (the pastor God used to switch my vocation from business to pastoral ministry), Nancy is the developer and author of the Study Guide. Along with many others, I've learned so much from hearing and watching men and women involved in the growth of the prayer movement–C. Peter Wagner, Cindy Jacobs, Chuck Pierce, and so many others. Surely, the Body of Christ is an incredible thing!

I also want to thank Pam Ikasalo who has labored with my handwritten pages to get it all typed, corrected, re-typed—a seemingly interminable task. You made what seems impossible a reality!

More than anyone else, I want to give credit for this book to my wife, Nancy. It was she who said, "We can't be successful in having people pray for Spain (our primary missions target beginning in 1992) unless we take them there to pray." Leading those teams of just-regular-folks into cities and plazas and overlooks spurred me to think more deeply and extensively about God's purpose for our prayers so that in turn I could help encourage our team to pray. And in her own praying, she continually modeled and models how to pray effectively. She was the first to push me to write this book as a way of spreading to a wider circle the insights that we've found helpful. And if you have the privilege of knowing her, it won't surprise you to learn that she never stopped reminding me: "You need to write this book!" Finally, Nancy, here it is.

But wait…I have one more acknowledgement. When I reflect on the process of discovery that has resulted in what I'm sharing in the pages of this book, I am overwhelmed by the very specific ways God has led me. Father, Son and Holy Spirit—to you alone belongs the highest praise. May your immense purposes be furthered by all you've revealed in this simple book.

INTRODUCTION

The reason behind this book is pretty simple: all of us have been given a fantastic privilege to pray— not for religious *points*, but for God-authored *results*. Prayer is so incredibly powerful; and yet so often for so many it feels incredibly weak, and so prayer drifts to the bottom of our To-Do List (and doesn't even make our Must Do List). We *intend* to pray of course…we just don't get around to doing it very often.

My experience growing up in the church (a really good church through which God did much to shape my life) was that prayer got a lot of *exhortation* ("You need to pray regularly"), and *admiration* ("She is a real prayer warrior!"), but not a lot of *explanation* ("Let me show you why prayer is so important, in fact essential…").

This book is written out of my own need for practical explanations and encouragements to pray. It contains significant insights from Scriptures and experiences I and others have had that have helped me embrace prayer in deeper, more fulfilling, and persistent ways. As I have shared them with others, they have found them encouraging as well.

I believe it can do the same for you. If you are someone who is already committed to prayer, I believe this book will be a tremendous source of encouragement for and expansion of that commitment. For those for whom prayer is something you do because you know you *should*, for whom prayer is more of a duty than a privilege and access to God's power and life—I believe God will use this book to release you from law into the freedom of grace. I believe your *experience* of prayer will change as your *understanding* of prayer changes. Finally, this book is for those of you who are just exploring what this thing called prayer really is. I believe it will give you a deeply-laid foundation upon which you can begin to build a wonderful, God-designed life of bringing the Kingdom rule of God into every circumstance of this world. For that God-given mission, prayer is uniquely essential. This book will help you see why that is true and how you can be increasingly effective in doing it.

Frank Laubach considered himself a pretty ordinary person who set himself a simple—but in his experience of Christianity—a pretty extraordinary goal: to pray about everything throughout the course of every day. Some years later he wrote to share his experience as a practical encouragement to others.

He perfectly expresses what I hope this book will accomplish:

> "In writing about prayer one ought to be practical and not just theoretical. It is not enough to tell people how necessary it is to pray. They want to know how they can pray. Praying is the most difficult thing in the world for most people most of the time. They may start a method of praying for a while, but they give it up after a brief effort. People need to know what kind of prayer can last through a lifetime. Some kinds of prayer will work when we are in the mood, or when we are in a foxhole. But a real Christian will not be satisfied to pray only on occasions. You and I want a type of prayer that stays with us and is as workable on ordinary days as it is in the depths of despair. We are sure that prayer ought to be as much a common day-by-day practice as eating or breathing.
>
> We all believe that. But for most people it is for emergencies or church services only. They do not like it to be that way and they do not admit it to others but they know it deep down in their soul. They want the answer to this question:
>
> 'Have I missed a kind of prayer that goes with me all day every day for a lifetime?'"
>
> -Frank Laubach, *Man of Prayer* (Syracuse, NY: Laubach Literacy International, 1990), p.327

This book presumes you—as I have done for years—are asking that question. It presumes that—like me—you want prayer to be a real part of your real life. It presumes that you're willing to do more than read about prayer; and that you're hoping God will help you because, if it's all up to you, you're pretty sure you'll never really succeed. It presumes you want to succeed. It presumes you want to grow in prayer. It presumes God wants this more than we do and will help us!

And that's where this book really begins: with God's vision of us and for us…

CHAPTER ONE

Our Name is House of Prayer

One of the final public acts of Jesus' ministry was overturning the tables of the money changers and driving them from the temple in Jerusalem. His explanation? "It is written, 'My Father's house shall be called a house of prayer for all the nations'" (Mark 11:15).

I have never been a person who loves to pray in the same way as I love to go out to eat with a few good friends, or to read a good book, or to go body surfing, or to teach or worship. There are times when I genuinely love to read the Bible—to feel my understanding deepen, to suddenly see how one thing connects to something else, to meditate on or discuss with others how what God says applies to me and my life. But I've never loved to pray like that.

That's not to say I haven't had some wonderful encounters with God in prayer—because I have—or that I don't experience great satisfaction after many times of prayer. It's just most of my experiences of prayer are based on faith. That is, I pray because of what I *believe* the results will be, not because of what happens to me every time I pray. I have to overcome a resistance to praying by persuading myself of its good effects. I need to be encouraged to pray.

I have found that most people are like me. But what I have also discovered is that God wants to and will encourage us to pray—by giving us reasons we can use to persuade ourselves to pray. We can count on it because of what God has revealed about His purpose for our lives. One of those places of revelation is this well-known event when Jesus cleared out the temple.

To grasp its full implication for you and me, we need to grasp the context within which Jesus was acting and then speaking. Think for a moment about the experience of two of Israel's greatest prophets: Ezekiel and Isaiah.

Ezekiel describes something the Lord told him to do:

> "Now, son of man, take a clay tablet, put it in front of you and draw the city of Jerusalem on it. Then lay siege to it: erect siege works against it, build a ramp up to it, set up camps against it and put battering rams around it. Then take an iron pan, place it as an iron wall between you and the city and turn your face toward it. It will be a sign to the house of Israel. Then lie on your left side and put the sin of the house of Israel upon yourself. You are to bear their sin for the number of days you lie on your side. I have assigned you the same number of days as the years of their sin. So for 390 days you will bear the sin of the house of Israel. After you have finished this, lie down again, this time on your right side, and bear the sin of the house of Judah. I have assigned you 40 days, a day for each year. Turn your face toward the siege of Jerusalem and with bared arm prophesy against her. I will tie you up with ropes so that you cannot turn from one side to the other until you have finished the days of your siege."
>
> Ezekiel 4:1–8, NIV

Imagine being there in Assyria (present day Iraq) with Ezekiel as one of thousands of Jewish refugees forced to leave your homeland. Imagine watching Ezekiel in his front yard setting up a brick, building a little fort, fashioning miniature battering rams and tiny siege mounds.

Imagine the conversations.

"What's Ezekiel doing?"

"Laying in his front yard pointing at a brick"

"Still? How long has he been out there?"

"About four months so far."

The Lord was using his prophet Ezekiel to speak without speaking—to communicate a message without reducing the message to words. In Ezekiel's actions, God was speaking to the Jewish refugees and to those still living in Jerusalem.

Ezekiel is not the only prophet called to speak without words. Two hundred years before, Isaiah was called to do something even more embarrassing.

> "In the year that the commander came to Ashdod, when Sargon the king of Assyria sent him and he fought against Ashdod and captured it, at that time the Lord spoke through Isaiah the son of Amoz, saying, 'Go and loosen the sackcloth from your hips and take your shoes off your feet.' And he did so, going naked and barefoot. And the Lord said, 'Even as My servant Isaiah has gone naked and barefoot three years as a sign and token against Egypt and Cush, so the king of Assyria will lead away the captives of Egypt and the exiles of Cush, young and old, naked and barefoot with buttocks uncovered, to the shame of Egypt. Then they shall be dismayed and ashamed because of Cush their hope and Egypt their boast. So the inhabitants of this coastland will say in that day, Behold, such is our hope, where we fled for help to be delivered from the king of Assyria; and we, how shall we escape?'"
>
> Isaiah 20:1–6

God commanded Isaiah to take off his clothes and his shoes and walk around naked. How naked? So naked that his buttocks were uncovered. For three years.

The point of both these experiences is God's view of them, clearly stated here in verse 2: "the Lord *spoke through* Isaiah…" The literal Hebrew reads "spoke by the hand of…" conveying the sense: by Isaiah's actions, not his tongue.

A prophet is appointed to be a mouthpiece for God's revelation. Often we think of a prophet as someone who just repeats God's words or describes a picture God lets him (or her) see. But many times God wants His mouthpiece to display in some specific action a message. The prophet doesn't *describe* a picture…he *is* the picture.

Why do we, after giving our lives to Jesus Christ, get baptized in water? Because it is a thoroughly prophetic act. As we do it, we are a living picture of Jesus' death, burial and resurrection. It is a *public* action which depicts a prophetic revelation from God about what has happened to us. We are "saying" to principalities and powers in heavenly places, and to human witnesses: I am identified with Jesus. His cross has achieved another victory on earth. There is another living agent of God's Kingdom here amongst the forces of darkness.

Prophetic revelation, therefore, is not only *talking*; it is often *doing*. And in the doing God is both communicating something and accomplishing something—although in a symbolic, foreshadowing kind of a way.

This is the context within which Jesus spoke and acted during His earthly ministry. He was prophet, priest and king. He was capital "P" Prophet. He was *the* Prophet, as well as *the* Priest and *the* King. Throughout His life, Jesus did things which may have appeared to be simply things He did, when in actual fact He was acting as Prophet. His actions were a message from the Father revealing His view of reality and purpose.

The events leading up to, surrounding and including the cleansing of the temple are full of these kinds of prophetic actions. Immediately before entering the temple, Jesus rode into Jerusalem on a donkey.

As Matthew specifically tells us, this was a prophetic action fulfilling Zechariah's promise "See, your king comes to you, gentle and riding on a donkey" (Matthew 21:4–5, quoting Zechariah 9:9).

The point is that Jesus rides into Jerusalem on a donkey not because that was the animal that happened to be available, but because riding a donkey communicated a message. A conquering king would ride in on a warhorse, not a donkey. One day, Jesus will ride in on a horse. It will be the day of battle where every enemy is put to death. That event is pictured by John in Revelation 19:

> "I saw heaven standing open and there before me was a white horse, whose rider is called Faithful and True. With justice he judges and makes war. His

eyes are like blazing fire, and on his head are many crowns… On his robe and on his thigh he has this name written": KING OF KINGS AND LORD OF LORDS."

Revelation 19:11, 12, 16

But in A.D. 30 he rode a donkey to signify that he comes in humility inviting his enemies to receive him and become his friends. It is a prophetic act immediately preceding his entering the temple and throwing out the moneychangers.

And immediately following the temple incident, Matthew describes what happened when Jesus re-entered Jerusalem the following day:

"Early in the morning, as he was on his way back to the city, he was hungry. Seeing a fig tree by the road, he went up to it but found nothing on it except leaves. Then he said to it. 'May you never bear fruit again!' Immediately the tree withered. When the disciples saw this, they were amazed. 'How did the fig tree wither so quickly?' they asked."

Matthew 21:18–20

Jesus responded to their question and answered, "By faith." But the disciples in an important sense were asking the wrong question. They thought the point was, "How do you wither fig trees?" The real question was "Why did you curse that fig tree (and so of course it withered)?"

The disciples wrongly assumed they knew the answer to the "Why" question: Jesus was hungry. Their reasoning looks like this:

Jesus is hungry ^{therefore} He looks for fruit on the fig tree… but, the fig tree is barren ^{therefore} Jesus curses the fig tree and it withers.

Looked at this way, Jesus' response to the barren fig tree is like that of a spoiled child: If I can't have what I want, I'll make sure no one else can get anything either! This doesn't seem like the same man who wept over Jerusalem because they refused to follow him.

As a way to understand what's really going on, think of a different outcome:

Jesus is hungry ^{therefore} He looks for fruit on the fig tree… But, the fig tree is barren ^{therefore} Jesus commands fruit to appear. It does: he eats and is satisfied. (His disciples still ask, "How did you do that?...)

Does this seem more like the Jesus revealed in the New Testament? Not exactly! You might remember the situation Jesus confronted at the start of his ministry when Satan encouraged him to turn stones into bread to satisfy his hunger after 40 days of fasting. Why Jesus refused then is the reason why this does not fit the fig tree episode either. There are three principles the disciples' apparent understanding of things would violate.

The first is that Jesus never used the power of miracles to benefit himself. The gift was always exercised for the sake of others. His own hunger or thirst always required him to be dependent on someone else.

The second is that the faith Jesus spoke of and exercised was faith in God, not "the Force". A faith that taps into "the Force" imagines the kind of power released by the Sorcerer's Apprentice. You remember the story, or maybe the Walt Disney animated version in "Fantasia" where Mickey Mouse is the Sorcerer's Apprentice. The Sorcerer leaves his apprentice to mop the floor of the laboratory. The Apprentice has a great idea: why not use magic to cause the mop to come alive and do the work? The problem is that he can get the mop to start, but he can't get it to stop. And when he finally tries to stop it for good by chopping it in two with an axe, both halves become furiously working mops. He chops both of them in two—but now there are four mops working away. And so on and so on, until the laboratory is overrun with scores of mops and flooded with buckets of water, and the Sorcerer returns to call a halt to the Apprentice's mess.

This mistaken idea of faith is that power is available for whatever Jesus wants to do at any moment. But the faith Jesus spoke of is very different. It is faith in His Father. Jesus says, "I can do nothing of myself, unless it is something I see the Father doing; for whatever the *Father* does, these things the Son does in like manner" (John 5:19).

The faith Jesus described is faith in a Person, not a Force. True faith that moves mountains or withers a fig tree is *Person*-al faith. It is faith that operates exactly as Jesus did in this event. Here's what went on:

Jesus was alerted by feeling hunger as he approached a fig tree. In his heart, he was asking, "Father, is this You?" Although he knew very well that it wasn't the right season for figs, he went over to the tree and checked.

As he did, he knew that the Father was right in the middle of this event. He sensed the Father's decree: "Let this fig tree be cursed."

Jesus also knew what this meant: the fig tree symbolized the nation of Israel. He knew their opportunity to respond to his invitation to repent, receive the kingdom of God and so "bring forth fruit" was at an end. Because as a nation they had rejected him, God was revealing the imminent result—as a nation they would be cursed and withered.

To go back to the disciples' question, instead of asking "How did the fig tree wither so quickly?" they should have asked, "Why did the Father want the fig tree withered? What is He saying to us?"

The point that has significance for us is that, like the preceding incident of the choice of a donkey, this incident of the fig tree is also a prophetic act. Both events are messages conveyed by what Jesus does.

In exactly the same way, the event sandwiched in between these two prophetic acts is prophetic. It combines words and works to communicate God's message. To understand that message, we need to pay attention to both what Jesus says and what he does.

This is the event as Matthew records it:

> "And Jesus entered the temple, and cast out all those who were buying and selling in the temple, and overturned the tables of the moneychangers and the seats of those who were selling doves. And He said to them, 'It is written, My house shall be called a House of Prayer, but you are making it a robbers' den.' And the blind and the lame came to Him in the temple, and He healed them.'"
>
> Matthew 21:12–14

Jesus did something or spoke something concerning the temple only three times in the Gospel accounts. (There is a fourth indirect allusion in John 7, which promises the Holy Spirit to every believer and links its fulfillment to Ezekiel's vision of a river flowing from God's new temple). One is in Matthew 24, Mark 13 and Luke 21, when his disciples are admiring the temple. It *was* a tremendous architectural achievement, and was one of the seven wonders of the Roman Era. The disciples, I'm sure, were thinking in terms of Jesus taking over Israel, establishing God's Kingdom and giving them authority over that beautiful temple.

Jesus looks at them, looks at the temple, and says to their amazement, "Not one stone of these great buildings will be left upon another and not torn down."

A second temple incident is recorded in John 2. Jesus drives out those selling sacrificial animals, and is asked, "What sign do you show us as your authority for doing these things?" Here's the ensuing dialogue with John's commentary on its meaning:

> "Jesus answered and said to them, 'Destroy this temple, and in three days I will raise it up.' The Jews then said, 'It took forty-six years to build this temple, and you will raise it up in three days?'
> But He was speaking of the temple of His body. So when He was raised from the dead, His disciples remembered that He said this; and they believed the Scripture and the word Jesus had spoken."
>
> John 2: 19–20

In both these instances, Jesus predicts "the destruction of the temple." In the first instance, He means the Jewish temple. In the second, He means His own body. He uses the same language to describe both, because in God's way of looking at things the two things are inextricably related. They are much more similar than they are different. The Jewish temple building, which is the successor to the original tabernacle, is a pictorial preview of the real temple built by God from a living, breathing person. The physical temple points to the real temple: Jesus.

The temple, of course, was originally conceived by David and built by Solomon. David received a blueprint of what the temple should look like (see 1 Chronicles 28: 9–19), just as Moses had received a blueprint of what the tabernacle should look like (Exodus 25: 8-9, Exodus 39: 42–43). The temple replaced and fulfilled the same function as the tabernacle. The tabernacle was a moving place of God's dwelling while Israel was a people on the move. The temple was a fixed place of God's dwelling when Jerusalem came under Israel's control. Both the tabernacle and the temple were meant for *the* place (not merely *a* place) where God would dwell among men.

Yet, when David first thought about building the temple, God responded with a clue about the significance of the temple.

> "You shall not build a house for me to dwell in…
> [Instead, I,] the Lord will build a house for you. It
> shall come about when your days are fulfilled that
> you must go to be with your fathers, that I will set
> up one of your descendants after you, who shall be
> of your sons; and I will establish his kingdom. He
> shall build for me a house. I will be his father and he
> will be my son; and I will not take my lovingkindess
> away from him…but I will settle him in my house
> and in my kingdom forever, and his throne shall be
> established forever."
>
> 1 Chronicles 17: 4, 10–12

On one level of meaning, God was affirming that the temple would be His dwelling—His place of residence in the same way our homes are our places of residence. And He was affirming that even though David would not be permitted to build this temple, that God would make David "at home" in the land he had conquered for the Jewish nation, and that one of David's sons would be empowered to build the temple. Again, on this first level of meaning, the son empowered to build the temple was Solomon. But there is clearly a second level of meaning in God's response. The builder of the temple would be descended from David's sons, a son of God, settled in God's house and God's kingdom forever, given rulership over that kingdom as king forever.

While Solomon did build the temple, he did not fulfill all that God said. Rather, God was making it clear that both Solomon and the temple he built were pointers to the real temple. So when Jesus spoke of the temple in the way he did, he was drawing attention to God's second level of meaning; I will let your son Solomon build a temple, and it will be the place of my dwelling, because my intention has always been to have a dwelling on the earth among men, and Solomon's temple will represent that reality and continually point to that reality before and until it comes. And when Jesus said "Destroy this temple, and in three days I will raise it up," He was saying that God's original and ultimate purpose was about to be fulfilled. He was saying, "I am the promised descendant empowered to build the real temple, and the real temple is not a building but a person, me, my body."

Later, Jesus is referring to this reality when he calls himself "the stone…the chief cornerstone" (Matthew 21:42). And it is why both Paul and Peter describe God's salvation as individual people being built by the Holy Spirit into "a holy temple…a dwelling of God…Christ Jesus Himself being the cornerstone" (Ephesians 2: 20–22, 1 Peter 2: 4–7).

When Jesus says, "Destroy this temple, and in three days I will raise it up," He is saying, "I am the *real* temple. This temple you will destroy when you crucify me; but this temple will be re-erected when three days later I am resurrected." Jesus, together with all who believe and receive him, is the temple.

Therefore, when Jesus enters the temple (in Matthew 21), throws out the moneychangers and says, "It is written, 'My house shall be called a House of Prayer,'" He was acting and speaking prophetically about the true temple—you and me. He was not merely getting a few moneychangers out of the temple for a few hours. He was revealing something about the future of the true temple *over which he has full authority*. And when he deliberately quotes Isaiah, saying, "My house shall be called a house of Prayer," he was naming the true temple. For us, names are not that significant. Our choice of a name for our children—or our parents' choice of a name for us—is usually based on someone in our family, or perhaps a respected friend, or simply a name that sounds good. God, however, views a name very differently. When the angel, Gabriel, appears to Joseph in a dream to explain that Mary's pregnancy has been caused supernaturally by the Holy Spirit, he also tells Joseph to name the child "Jesus", because "he will save his people from their sins." The name "Jesus" means "God saves." Throughout Scripture, whenever God names a person, or changes their name, it is because of the *meaning* of that name. God changes Abram to Abraham, Sarai to Sarah, Jacob to Israel, Saul to Paul. The reason is this: a name reveals a person's *function* and *destiny*. When Jesus says, "My house shall be called a House of Prayer," he is naming us. He is revealing our function and destiny. Would you call the church today a House of Prayer? Certainly it looks more like a House of Prayer in some places than in others. But the point is that it will become this, because God's naming is God's promise of fulfillment. In fact, the name has to do with the DNA—the genetic blueprint—designed and created by God, which determines the function and destiny of the mature person. The church—God's temple—has Jesus' DNA. He *was* a man of prayer. He *is* a man of prayer, continually interceding for "those who draw near to God through him" (Hebrews 7:25). Do you believe that?

Think for a moment about Jesus naming Peter. When Jesus first met him, his name was Simon, son of John. Jesus looked at him and said, "Your name will no longer be Simon, but you will be called Peter" (John 1:42). Why? Because the name, Peter, means "rock". How rock-like was Peter? How about when he stepped over the side of the boat and began walking on the water? Then, like a rock, he began to sink—but I don't think that's the kind of rock Jesus meant. How rock-like was Peter when Jesus told his disciples he was going to suffer and die? At that point, Peter actually "*rebuked*" Jesus, telling him that was a foolish and faithless plan, to which Jesus responded, "Get behind me Satan!" Or how rock-like was Peter when the young servant-girl suggested that he was one of Jesus' followers, and Peter began denying it with curses? Yet, Jesus wrote that name on Peter. Because that is what Peter became.

In the same way, Jesus has written the name House of Prayer, on us, his church. On you and me. How well do you accord with that name? No matter where we are as the church, no matter where you and I are as part of the Church, this is God's promised destiny for us. And knowing that is helpful! Everything in the Christian life occurs by faith. And faith has two sides to it. In order to have faith, you first have to acknowledge that where you are is not where God wants you to be. Therefore, you need Him to do something in you. The other side of faith is that you believe God wants to and will do it in you. It is faith in what God has promised. One of the most significant revelations of this is found in Deuteronomy 26:29. "The secret things belong to the Lord our God, but the things revealed belong to us and to our sons forever..." A *revealed* promise belongs to us. We can be assured that God wants to and will release whatever is necessary to make it happen. But we must actively exercise our faith! It starts with looking at our hearts and saying, "I don't see that name written on my heart yet. And as the church I'm part of, I don't see that name "House of Prayer" yet written over it." That's actually the first step of faith. The next step is to say, "And Lord, I believe that you want to and will do that in me and in us. Lord, I need your help—will you help me?" Then we can expect to hear the Lord say, "All right...will you go and pray today?" That is always faith's third step: acting on what God's promise is.

Faith does not normally begin with an overwhelming desire to do something. Faith for prayer does not normally begin with us *wanting* to pray. It begins with God asking, "Will you pray?" About five years after moving to Kingston, Massachusetts to start the church I pastor, we realized that we had a hard time building teams because we had church made up of independent, New England entrepreneurs. (I guess I attracted people with a bit of my own genetic code...) They had their own businesses because they hated working for someone else who could tell them what to do and when. Being an entrepreneur, a pioneer, a self-starter, is a good thing—it just has some potential weaknesses. One big one is a stubborn resistance to authority. Any authority. Including God's authority. I remember one of our key leaders sharing an experience he'd had the night before. He'd been realizing that he did not have a submissive heart, and that it was blocking his growth as a disciple of Jesus. As he was getting ready to get into bed, he picked up a magazine from the dresser across the room. About three or four steps from his bed, he felt like the Lord said, "Dave, why not read the Bible instead?" His immediate response was, "The Bible?...Lord, I'd rather read this magazine." He took another step towards the bed and heard the Lord say, "Dave, Dave, Dave..." He threw the magazine down and angrily picked up his Bible. Then he thought he heard the Lord say, "How about getting the dictionary." So he pulled his dictionary from the bookshelf. As he did, the Lord spoke to him again: "I want you to look up the definition of "submission"...then "docile", then "meek". That was the beginning of a real breakthrough in his deeply-ingrained heart attitudes. It is what happens if we are willing to say, "Lord, this is where I am—and I see it is not where I'm supposed to be. I know what you want to do in me, and what you promise to do in me. Even though I don't feel like I want it...I'm willing." That is what God is looking for in you and me—a willingness to have the name, House of Prayer, written on our hearts.

To be honest, there's a whole lot of resistance to having that word written in us! There's the initial resistance that comes from ignorance and apathy. We read this or hear this truth about us being God's House of Prayer, and we don't recognize or understand how incredibly important it is. So our enemy, as Jesus describes in the parable of the sower, steals that truth from us. We just forget about it. We remember we read something or heard something—but we can't quite recall what it was. It never takes root; and it never bears fruit.

Think about the moment Jesus spoke to Peter about following him and being trained to become a fisher of men. What Peter immediately realized was that that invitation meant giving up his business, giving up his home, giving up his property, giving up his retirement package, giving up his family. What about us? We hear Jesus' invitation like this: "I've forgiven your sins by dying on the cross. Will you accept me as your Lord and Savior?" So often we say, "Oh, yes, thank you. Thank you for forgiving me." And we walk on. We walk away. We don't realize what Jesus wants to do in us. We don't realize that He wants to write His name on our hearts so that we become like him, we follow him, we listen to him, we do his work…whatever that might mean.

Jesus is saying, "My house shall be called a House of Prayer." This is part of his invitation. And it means we will be called to pray. We're going to have to do prayer rather than do other things. We have a certain amount of available time. There are times we want to relax, and God says, "Pray." There are times we want to go and earn a few extra dollars, and God says, "No, I need you to go and pray." It takes commitment to follow the Lord's direction. And we begin to realize that if the name, House of Prayer, is going to be written on my heart, I'm going to have to give up parts of my life I'm not sure I want to give up.

Choices and consequences. I believe when Jesus, as recorded in verse 12, came into the temple and "overturned the tables of the money changers and the seats of those who were selling doves," he did it because the House of Prayer had become something else. It stands as a warning to us as well.

If our church is a house of prayer, we will be focused on the heart of what it means to be in the Kingdom of God—that God is the initiator of what we do and the source of what we need. If anything needs to be done, God must be our provision. If we're doing things God hasn't initiated, and if God isn't empowering us to do them, we're not going to accomplish anything. The danger of God's blessing is that we shift the focus of our dependence to what we already have instead of the One who blesses. The result of that choice over time is the lesson of the money changers. We begin to focus on people—people's actions, people's energies, people's power and intellect and money. And God is saying, "You keep the name 'Church', but in depending on the strength of people you are in fact robbing Me. You are drawing people in, drawing finances in, drawing in time and energy, but you are using it for yourself, for *your* programs, for *your* interests. So you are making My house 'a den of robbers.'"

By *praying*, we instead are depending on Him to initiate, empower and provide. The result is all we receive gets drawn into the work of *God*, into the purposes of God for us, into what God is doing and Holy Spirit is building.

The final part of this prophetic act in the temple is described in verse 14: "And the blind and the lame came to Him in the temple and He healed them."

That is what happens when we take seriously being the House of Prayer!

I think of it this way: When the church becomes the House of Prayer, we no longer set up eye charts for the blind and strength tests for the lame at our front door. We welcome them to meet the Healer.

Here's the typical church eye chart: Do you believe there is a God? (Yes). How about line 2—Do you believe Jesus is the Son of God? (Yes, I think I see that). Then there's line 3—Do you believe the Bible is God's fully inspired Word? (That's a bit hazy…). How about the next line, then—Do you read the Bible every day? (Well…). What? I'm sorry, you can't come in here unless you do…or at least are willing to pretend you do.

I think there are a few more lines on that eye test, depending on the particular denomination we're part of. But there's also the strength test for the lame: How is your walk? A good answer would be: I'm doing well in my job; my marriage and family is in order; I have my quiet time; I don't drive over 55.

In man's house, we worry about the regulations. In God's house, the blind and lame are welcomed. If you're blind—come here. If you have problems with your walk—you've just been fired, your family is trashed, you don't know where you're going next—come here. Jesus will heal your blindness and your lameness.

In all honesty, I have never prayed for someone who is blind and have them see. I know people who've done that—but I haven't. Someday

I want to do that, and I believe I will. Nor have I ever prayed for someone who is crippled in a wheelchair and seen them healed and walking. I know people who've done that—but I haven't. I once sat behind a girl in her twenties who'd been severely injured in a motorcycle accident and had to use braces to walk. I saw her miraculously healed, not just walking, but running without her braces. I've prayed for at least four people I can remember and name who were severely "lame" because of problems in their backs and seen them fully healed and pain free.

But I have seen the Lord come again and again and open people's blind eyes to the truth that Jesus lives and wants to save them. And I am seeing people every day being healed of the terrible lameness in their lives. That counts!

What Jesus' prophetic act in Matthew 21 encourages me to do is to believe that as we become the House of Prayer, what we will experience more and more of is His power to heal and to save. The more we become the House of Prayer, the more we will see it. The less of the House of Prayer we are, the less we'll see. I'm encouraged to pray!

CHAPTER 2

When Shall I Pray?

All my life I have admired and aspired to become like men and women who prayed a lot. I think of Dr. James Dobson telling the story of his father wearing off the tops of his shoes before wearing out the soles because he spent so much time kneeling in prayer. I think of Rees Howells who was told by his doctor to stop praying so long with such intensity because he was literally wearing out his heart. But he couldn't stop and didn't stop and died "of a broken heart"—broken in desperate prayer for those in desperate need of God's intervention.

I love and am inspired by Cindy Jacobs' description of an unknown woman, Vinita Copeland, who inspired her to pray. Every morning she got up at 4 am, went down into her basement and prayed. She prayed for friends. She prayed for her family. Over the years, she prayed for thousands of men, women and children whose needs had been sent to her asking that she pray. One day one of her relatives looked down and said, "Vinita, is what the matter with your knees? They look like camel knees." She answered that she was praying for her son. At that time he was running from God as fast as he could go. The relative said, "Well, Vinita, can't you pray standing up?" But she couldn't and she didn't stop kneeling as she prayed.

Cindy Jacobs recounts one day visiting her home and going with her into the basement where she prayed:

> "I noticed a little pallet with a shoebox on it to one side. I asked her 'Nonnie (her nickname), what's that pallet over there?' She answered, 'Darlin', that's where I pray.' The presence of the Lord washed over me as I

knelt down on the pallet and picked up the shoebox overflowing with pictures. 'Nonnie,' I asked, 'what are these?' 'Those are my prayer pictures.' 'Who are they?' 'I don't know most of them,' she said. 'People send me pictures of their loved ones to pray over.' She went on to explain that she would pray over them until God said, *it's done*. And then she would stop. There were tear stains on those pictures of people she did not even know...At the end of her life when she entered the gates of heaven, her body was literally worn out from her years of intercessory prayer."

Possessing The Gates of the Enemy, pp. 78–79

But I have not become like Vinita Copeland, or Rees Howells, or even Dr. Dobson's father. My personal opinion is that God calls some people to a *ministry of prayer*. He calls everyone to *minister in prayer*. And there's a difference.

Those called to a *ministry of prayer* will be able to spend large amounts of time praying, and will discover a *fulfilling satisfaction* from doing just that.

What I mean is this: From my earliest childhood until I was thirty, I had a strong desire to be involved in theater, music and media. As an intentional disciple of Jesus, I became involved in these things with the goal to communicate the Gospel to our culture. I went to school for this. As a short-term missionary in Africa, I worked at this. Together with a close friend, I began a company to further this. I loved using media to reach the lost and train the found. It was clearly my call and my *ministry*. No matter *how* much I wore myself out doing it, I had a *fulfilling satisfaction* in it.

At the age of thirty, a series of circumstances ultimately brought me to a place of believing that God was asking me to yield up this ministry in the way that He asked Abraham to give up his son, Isaac. As I did, the passion for media died. It wasn't a gradual diminishing—it was completely gone overnight.

For the next seven years, I struggled to discover what—if anything—would replace it. Often I wondered if perhaps it might not be replaced, but resurrected. Gradually, without my being aware of it for a very long time, I was actually finding the same kind of fulfilling satisfaction from teaching the Bible. At the end of those seven years, I finally recognized what God had done. I left the media business for good, and have devoted my life since to the business of teaching and preaching.

My point is that the kind of examples of men and women given to prayer that have always impacted me are examples of people called to a *ministry of prayer*. God uses them to call others to that ministry. But all are *not* called to the ministry of prayer.

For those who aren't, God uses these examples to encourage the rest of us to honor and utilize these gifted people. And also He uses them to encourage us to use our time and energy to *minister in prayer*.

Not all of us are evangelists; but all of us need to honor and utilize those who are, as well as to "do the work of an evangelist" ourselves (2 Timothy 4:5). Not all of us are prophets; but all of us need to honor and utilize those who are, as well as to prophecy ourselves—"for you can all prophesy" (1 Corinthians 14:31).

Here is the bottom line: if you are called to the ministry of prayer—we need you and God needs you to step up and fulfill your call. The hours I spend in study and preparation to fulfill my call to teach, you need to set aside to pray. But if you are not called to the *ministry* of prayer, you—like me—are called to minister in prayer.

Understanding this has helped me in two important ways. First, it has released me from the guilt of false expectations. I don't need to feel guilty if I'm not praying two or three or four hours a day—or most days. Second, it frees me to ask, "Lord, when *should* I pray? How should I understand prayer in relation to all the other things I'm called to do?"

There are three particular passages of Scripture that have shaped my perspective on the answer to those questions.

The first is in Mark 9 and tells the story of Jesus returning from the mountain where he met with Moses and Elijah, and where his body and clothes were temporarily transformed into a state of glory. He discovers that the disciples he left behind are confused and in trouble. They had tried unsuccessfully to cast a demon out of a boy. The father is upset, a crowd is gathering, and the disciples are frustrated. Jesus, of course, expels the demon and restores the boy to his thankful father. The disciples, however, are more frustrated than ever, and when they are able to get Jesus alone, they ask what they were embarrassed to ask in public: "Why couldn't we drive it out?"

Jesus responds, "This kind cannot come out by anything but prayer."

Think for a moment about his answer in the context of what had just taken place:

Jesus comes down from the mountain. He is confronted by the demonized boy's father who says, "Here's my boy. Your disciples have tried but failed to cast the demon out of him. What's going on here? Can *you* cast it out?"

Somehow, Jesus as he looks at the boy and assesses what has happened recognized exactly what he told his disciples: This kind of demon only comes out by prayer. But, does Jesus drop to his knees and begin to pray?

No! He simply speaks to the demon, saying, "Come out," and it comes out.

Yet, if this kind only comes out by prayer, when did Jesus pray?

He prayed early that morning. He prayed yesterday evening. He prayed the morning before that, the day before that, and the day before that. He often, the gospel accounts tell us, withdrew by himself to pray.

Think of this story from the point of view of the frustrated disciples. What do you suppose had happened when the father brought the boy to them? They would have said to the father, "Of course we can cast out this demon. We've seen Jesus do it, and we've done it ourselves just as he told us to." They would have looked intently into the young boy's eyes and sternly commanded, "In the name of Jesus of Nazareth, out!"

And, of course, nothing would have happened. Except that perhaps the boy would have been thrown to the ground, grinding his teeth, rolling his eyes and frothing at the mouth, as the demon in the boy mocked the powerless disciples.

Now what? If I were Bartholomew, say, and you were Nathanael, I'd look at you hoping you'd do something. You'd look at me hoping *I'd* do something. And at some point one of us, at least, would start to *pray*! "O God, help us! O Lord, come to our aid! Help us, Lord! God, help! We pray in the name of your Son, help this little child here."

Admittedly, this is reading between the lines. But I think we can be pretty sure given the situation—THEY WERE PRAYING!

When they finally were able to ask Jesus to explain, and heard his answer, they didn't respond "Hey! We *were* praying. A lot!" No. They understood that Jesus was saying to them, "You haven't *been* praying. Before you get to the power encounter, you must have already been praying."

This same principle is revealed when Jesus stands in front of the tomb where Lazarus has been buried just before the power encounter with death. Before commanding Lazarus to "come forth," Jesus prays these words: "Father, I thank You that You have heard Me. I knew that You always hear Me; but because of the people standing around I said it, so that they may believe that You sent Me" (John 11:41–42).

Notice the past tense "You *have heard* (already)…I *knew* (already)…" He could not say that if He hadn't been praying *in advance* of the event.

The point Jesus makes is that, in both situations, he had prayed beforehand so that he was ready for what He ultimately needed God's power to do.

The House of Prayer starts long before we see the power. For many of the situations we face today, only yesterday's prayer will do. For many situations, to begin to pray when we encounter the problem is to begin too late. Although we may not have the ministry of prayer, all of us must minister in prayer.

To minister means very simply to serve. To minister in prayer simply means to serve God by praying. I serve by worshiping Him in prayer. I serve by thanking Him in prayer. I serve by listening for His instructions in prayer. I serve by asking that His kingdom come and His will be done in the people and situations for which He wants me to pray.

This is not a formula, a one-to-one kind of ratio between prayer time and power given. It is a *principle of partnership*. As we serve God in praying, we are learning what it means to be his partner. We are learning what his heart is like and what his will really is. We are also learning to hear his voice—becoming alert to impressions or pictures or thoughts that come into our minds. This "partnership learning" can happen because as we are praying, we are disciplining ourselves to focus on God.

Certainly there are (thankfully!) many times when God sovereignly comes on us and gives us power without preceding prayer. But as His partnership people, He uses prayer to draw us into His partnership. His partnership people have learned how to partner with Him at times other than when a crisis comes. God is a team player! Working with a team means that everyone communicates and has input. God wants to input to us, and even more amazingly covets our input in determining what he does. His purpose is to have such a partnership people on earth who having prayed are able to confront every situation with the power of God. Without prayer the Body of Christ will face crises and be unable to see God's power released because we've not spent the time in prayer learning how to partner with him. We will face the crisis blind, deaf, and dumb—unable to see God's perspective, unable to hear his voice telling us what to do, unable to speak what he longs to say.

Therefore, these words of Jesus have been a great encouragement to me "to pray before I get there." And because I often don't know when I'm going to get there (crises usually seem to happen by surprise), I'm encouraged to pray *today*. The crisis may come this afternoon—and then it will be too late to start praying!

But, Lord, I thought Your power is available to anyone who asks at anytime.

And He answers: "Yes, it is...but there is something larger I'm working on. It is an eternal partnership with My people."

Andrew Murray once wrote:

> "The great thought of God was...to train man for the place he is to have with Christ upon the throne. God's purpose was that man should so rule that God would do nothing but through him, and that man should understand that he would do nothing but through God. It is in this wonderful relationship that prayer has its mystery and its glory."

The State of The Church, pg. 129

There is a second passage of Scripture that has helped me to understand *when* I should pray and *how* I should undertake prayer in relation to everything else I'm called to do. It's found in the very practical letter written by Jesus' brother James—leader for many years of the church in Jerusalem. (And let me substitute words that elaborate on what he means by "lust" and "murder").

> "You really want something and do not have it [lust]; so you step over and cheat other people to get it [murder]. You are envious and cannot obtain; so you fight and quarrel. You do not have because you do not ask…Is anyone among you suffering? Then he needs to pray.
> Is anyone cheerful? He is to sing praises."
>
> James 4:2 and 5:13

The sentence that has been so important to me is, "You do not have because you do not ask." What a slap in the face!

From God's perspective, we look at things we want and go after them in our own strength. In the face of a crisis—large or small—when we recognize something we really need, instead of immediately going to God and asking Him in prayer, we take things into our own hands. I try to get my wife to just SUBMIT! I try to manipulate circumstances to get a raise. I buy a lottery ticket. I privately poll the members of the board, letting them know a few negative things about the person I don't agree with. I do things to try to get my boss's attention hoping to make points.

There are thousands of things we do in a year to get—or try to get—what we want or need.

God says, you need to pray *at the moment*, throughout the process of your life.

Ask. Ask Me. Ask Me *when* you discover something you want. Prayer is meant to be an *always first* action.

If you begin suffering—first pray. And if you are feeling blessed by something—first praise (pray-se)!

I got to know Dr. Christy Wilson while I was a student at Gordon-Conwell Seminary. He had been a successful missionary in Afghanistan for many years until the government expelled him. When the Seminary offered him a position as professor of World Missions, he accepted with the provision that if Afghanistan ever opened up to Christian missionaries again, he would return. He was a man who understood prayer and praying. I soon learned that whoever shared a concern they were facing with Dr. Wilson, the response would always be, "Let's pray about that." And he would pray for it right there—wherever there happened to be. On the library steps. In the cafeteria line. *Whenever* was always incidental to *wherever*.

I realized that one thing could never be said about Christy Wilson: You have not because you ask not. And it has encouraged me to become one who prays whenever there is a need.

It's interesting how difficult it is to do this simple thing! Prayer is something we are quick to tell one another we *will* (in the undefined future) do for the need being shared right now. But I have found it surprisingly against the grain to pray about that need immediately.

During my days of study at Gordon-Conwell Seminary, the former President of that Seminary, and Pastor of Park Street Church in Boston, Dr. Harold John Ockenga, died. Our families had been long-term friends through my childhood and teenage years, and my wife and I were invited to the funeral held in the small congregational church nearby. Dr. Paul Toms—who had replaced Dr. Ockenga as Park Street's Pastor—and Billy Graham were scheduled to speak at the ceremony. The night before the funeral, I had a dream from which I awoke with a strong impression that I was to have Billy Graham pray for me to impart some of the spirit of evangelism resting on him.

This struck me as rather arrogant and more than rather improbable. But the impression wouldn't go away, so I told the Lord, if you give me a confirming sign and make an opportunity, I agree to ask him.

The next morning, we filed into the little New England church and found our seats. Billy Graham was nowhere to be seen.

At last, after everyone was in place, a black limousine pulled up at the front entrance, and Billy Graham stepped out and was escorted to the door by bodyguards.

So much for thinking of getting close to this famous man!

The service began. Hymns were sung. Prayers were offered. Billy Graham gave a remarkable tribute to Dr. Ockenga. Dr. Toms stood to give his address. As his text, he read from Mark, chapter 10.

> "Then they came to Jericho. And as He was leaving Jericho with His disciples and a large crowd, a blind beggar named Bartimaeus, the son of Timaeus, was sitting by the road. When he heard that it was Jesus

> the Nazarene, he began to cry out and say, 'Jesus, Son of David, have mercy on me!'
> Many were sternly telling him to be quiet, but he kept crying out all the more, 'Son of David, have mercy on me!'
> And Jesus stopped and said, 'Call him here.' So they called the blind man, saying to him, 'Take courage, stand up! He is calling for you.' Throwing aside his cloak, he jumped up and came to Jesus.
> And answering him, Jesus said, 'What do you want Me to do for you?' And the blind man said to Him, 'Rabboni, I want to regain my sight!' And Jesus said to him, 'Go; your faith has made you well.' Immediately he regained his sight and began following Him on the road."

In my entire life of funerals, I have never heard or even thought of using that story. I can no longer remember how those verses were applied to Dr. Ockenga—but I knew they certainly applied to me! If an angel had appeared, I couldn't have had a more clear confirmation: "Don, I respond to those willing to interrupt what God, Himself, may be doing in order to give them what they're desperate to receive. Will you act like the blind beggar Bartimaeus?"

Fortunately, (especially for Nancy, my wife sitting beside me) I accepted this as *confirmation* not an immediate action plan. I did not jump to my feet, interrupt the funeral and start shouting, "Billy Graham, please pray for me." What I did do was promise God that I would look for Him to give me a window of opportunity to ask Dr. Graham to pray for me.

The service ended. Billy Graham left the church and was escorted back into the limousine. The rest of us exited and made our way the relatively short distance to the graveside. I remember wondering if that Scripture had really been my confirmation; whether God had really wanted me to somehow get to Billy Graham before he left the church; whether this whole crazy idea was just a figment of my prideful imagination.

As we gathered at the graveside and waited, up from behind the site drove that black limousine. Out stepped Billy Graham. I told God I would look for His opportunity and take it if it came.

The short ceremony ended with Billy Graham offering a final benediction. I waited my turn to embrace the family. Two or three people went to shake hands with Billy Graham. This was my chance! The black limousine door was open, but Billy Graham was graciously speaking with each person wanting to meet him.

I took a breath and said something like this: "Hello, Dr. Graham. My name is Don Andreson and my family was close to the Ockengas for many years at Park Street Church. Two years ago, God called me out of business into full-time ministry. I'm just finishing up my studies here at Gordon-Conwell. You have a tremendous gift of evangelism, which New England desperately needs. Would you be willing to pray and ask God to place on me some of the Spirit He has given to you?"

As I began, he was shaking my hand and looking at me in a kindly way. As I made my request, he first looked at me intently, then nodded, saying, "Well, yes, I'll certainly pray for you." As he spoke, he was disengaging. Turning towards the open limousine door.

I said, "Dr. Graham. I mean would you pray for me right now? Would you pray and lay your hands on me? Right here?"

With a startled look, he turned to me. I don't know what thoughts were going through his mind, but clearly this was not a question he'd expected. He hesitated a fraction of a second, and then said, "Alright! I'll be happy to do that." He put his hand on my shoulder and prayed simply for what I'd asked.

The point of the story is not that I have become the next Billy Graham! Nor did Timothy become the next Apostle Paul—though Paul certainly laid hands on him and even mentored him. The point of the story is this:

1. God is the one who wanted prayer on the spot and arranged to make it happen. That is, God wants us to pray *whenever* the need arises. He wants us to *always first* pray.

2. Even Billy Graham finds it easier to put it off till an undefined later. There is a normal and natural resistance we find in ourselves to *not pray first*. This is something we need to determine to overcome.

3. I learned in an unforgettable way the incredible significance of the *present*. The future is not yet ours, and the past is no longer in our control. The only time available to us for sure is the present. Let's make it the time we first pray about whatever need becomes present. This is part of what makes us the House of Prayer.

The third passage of Scripture that has helped put the timing and extent of prayer into perspective is in Ephesians. Paul explains that all of us—whether we choose to or not—are locked in a great struggle between two kingdoms: the kingdom of God and the dominion of Satan, in whose hands the whole world lies (I John 5:19). Because this struggle is against rulers, powers, world forces of darkness and spiritual forces of wickedness in the heavenly places—and not against flesh and blood—our weapons cannot be bombs and bullets, but rather "spirit weapons" which have spiritual effect.

What can such weapons be?

First, Paul lists five components, which successfully will deflect the use of spiritual weapons against us, (truth, righteousness, God's peace, faith and God's salvation). Then he lists a sixth component. It's the only one that can be used to attack. This, says Paul, is "the sword of the Spirit;" that is, the word of God is a "spirit weapon." And, he continues, "With all prayer and petition *pray at all times* in the Spirit" (Ephesians 6:18).

Leaving aside for the moment what Paul means practically by the word of God and how it functions as a sword, just look at *when* he says to pray:…at all times.

In English, we could say, "Pray all the time," or "Pray always," or "Always be praying." Paul, however, wrote in Greek and used a word which has a very strong meaning that gives a different understanding. The phrase, "at all times" is *kairo* (*kairo* is the dative of *kairos*). Literally this means "in all times," where the word "times" means "the decisive moments," or "the decisive points of time." The word used here, *kairos*, is distinctly different from another word also meaning "time," the word *kronos*. From kronos we derive English words like chronology, chronic and chronicle. It means simply the process of time.

A helpful way to understand the difference in meaning between these two words is: we live through *kronos* time (chronological) until we find ourselves in a *kairos* time (decisive moment). When Jesus came announcing the kingdom of God, he used the word *kairos* when he said, "the *time* is fulfilled." A *kairos* moment is not just any old time; it is a decisive moment when God has brought many things together to accomplish a particular purpose.

Jesus, more than anyone, understood this and made it a practical part of the way he lived. Take one example when his brothers jeeringly told him to go on up to Jerusalem for the upcoming Feast of Booths so that he could "show [himself] to the world." Jesus replied, "My *time (kairos-decisive moment)* is not yet here…" (John 7:2–6). Shortly afterwards, he did travel to Jerusalem. The issue for Jesus was always, "Is it the *time* (*kairos*) to heal, or to speak, or to go to one city or another?"

The point for me is to reinforce in a powerful way the realization that we are meant to pray *every time* and *at the time* a specific need arises. Because we are God's people, God's servants, the hands and feet of Jesus Christ, God is arranging our *kronos* (chronological time) so that we arrive at His *kairos* (decisive moment) as the ones through whom He may accomplish His will. I can be confident that I am hearing this need from this person at this place because God wants me to pray about it right now. It's not just any old time; it's *kairos* time! It's God's appointed time!

What Paul is emphasizing when he says to "pray at all times," is that we, being in the very heart of the struggle Jesus began when he inaugurated the kingdom, should anticipate that our lives will be filled with all sorts of these *kairos* moments when, instead of putting it off to some better future time, we need to *pray*.

He adds, "in the Spirit." I'd like to share more about his "how" of praying at another point. But at this moment, it is enough to recognize we need to pray "listening" to the directions, impressions, and redirections of the Holy Spirit at all the times we pray. We're partners with God, himself!

CHAPTER 3

Prayer is Work

Bill Hybels once said that he can tell what a person's gift is by their response to his sermons. When he preaches on the great need for and impact of teaching, the person who comes up and says, "That was the best sermon you've ever preached" has the gift of teaching. When he preaches on evangelism, the person who comes up and says, "That's the best sermon!" has the gift of evangelism. The same holds true for prayer.

If you are reading this book, the likelihood is that you have a gift of prayer. And you will hopefully be encouraged to appreciate and expand the use of that gift.

But I'm really writing this for people who, like me, believe prayer is important but who find it a whole lot easier to do more and pray less. In arranging our days, we already have too little time to do the things we need to get done, (with enough time left over to do some things we like to do to relax and have fun).

I want to pass along something that has helped me perhaps more than anything else invest my time in prayer. But first a little background...

In 1992, I was invited to become involved in a partnership of Vineyard churches in New England whose goal was to develop a church-planting movement in Spain. The impetus for this came from Phil Strout who had been a church-planting missionary in Chile where he had heard God say, "The daughter needs to pray for the mother." He understood that to mean the nations of Latin and South America (Spain's daughters) should begin to pray for a release of Gospel in Spain (the mother). After encouraging that in the church he pastored, he returned to New England where he shared this vision with Vineyard churches there, and launched a missions partnership focused on Spain.

As our partnership was developing my wife, Nancy, and I were invited to become the prayer coordinators. As we thought about ways of getting as many as possible in our churches to pray for Spain, Nancy suggested that we organize annual Prayer Tours. Beginning in 1994 we have been taking teams of "normal" Christians to Spain with the primary purpose to pray in its streets and plazas.

Independent of us, Randy and Jacquie Chase, from the Palo Alto Vineyard, moved to Barcelona, Spain to start a church in 1992. As we joined forces, Randy decided to accompany us on one of our prayer tours. We were in the midst of our second week after prayer stops in Barcelona, Valencia and Grenada. It was early evening, and our team of around twenty had gathered at the site of an ancient Roman arch in Cordoba—a gateway to this city filled with so much history. There were a series of broad stone steps, forming a sort of mini-amphitheater rising up from the base of the arch to a street above. Most of the team was sitting on the steps, while some of us were standing at their base facing those seated. Randy was standing off to the side. We worshipped for a while, then began praying for God to come to Cordoba and to break into all Spain.

Here we were, a little group of unknown people, spending two weeks praying for a couple of hours once or twice a day in a few scattered cities. It was costing a couple thousand dollars per person to do this—and what were we accomplishing? These were the thoughts going through Randy's mind. The longer we prayed, the more frustrated he became. All this time and money spent on prayer seemed such a waste!

At that moment, Nancy began to pray. She was seated about a dozen rows up, toward the middle of the stone steps. Behind her, a foul-smelling man with wild eyes had sidled down from the street above and was muttering to himself with a glare fixed on the back of her head. Later, she told us that she just knew he was watching her, daring her to pray. She had to fight off a wave of nausea and fear and the certainty that if she prayed he would stand up and urinate on her. It took every ounce of determination to launch out in prayer no matter what might happen.

Randy, of course, knew none of this, but as Nancy began to pray, it was as if he was suddenly right in front of her—as though he was watching through a giant TV camera that zoomed in on Nancy's face. Randy knew it was God saying, "Pay attention!"

I was also standing at the base of the stairs. I wasn't paying much attention to the strange man, had no idea of what was going on in Nancy as she was praying, and was equally ignorant of what was happening to Randy. What I *did* have, was a growing sense that we were in the presence of some dark force that had "shut the door to the Gospel," and that was there mocking our attempts through prayer to open it wide. As Nancy finished praying, I began describing what I felt and declaring that we were here in the authority of Jesus—ruler of the nations—to open that closed window to the city of Cordoba. At that moment, I felt like I needed to confront the power that was mocking our prayers. (This is a little weird…) I began saying something like this: "And I say to you who have come to mock our prayers, you will no longer (and in my mind I'm debating about what word to use—this is all of course happening in micro-seconds or nano-seconds…*this* is the word I need to use) piss on this place, on this doorway, on this entrance for the Gospel."

As Nancy says whenever she tells the story: "Don *never* uses that word…*anywhere*…"

At that moment, the man behind Nancy stopped muttering, stood to his feet and walked up the steps. Nancy felt an immediate release from fear and nausea and shared with the rest of us what she'd just experienced.

Here is the point I want to make: in that experience, Randy realized that God was telling him to pay attention to the incredible importance of prayer. Yes, it is important to expend time and money on ways to share the gospel. Yes, it is important to expend time and money digging wells for clean water, caring for orphans and victims of AIDS, rescuing those caught in the sex trade—all in Jesus' name. But it is equally important to expend time and money on prayer!

And that is what both Old and New Testaments make quite clear.

In Paul's letter to his "son in the faith," Timothy, he gives him some "instructions." Why? Because, he writes, "May they help you fight well in the Lord's battles" (1 Timothy 1:18). That battle is for people, because "God our Savior…wants everyone to be saved and to understand the truth" (1 Timothy 2:4).

What are the instructions that will help Timothy fight this battle? "I urge you first of all, to pray…" In other words, before and as a vital part of getting done what God wants we need to pray.

In fact, after telling Timothy to "First of all…pray," and summarizing what the battle is about (to help people hear the message about Jesus who alone reconciles God and humanity) his next instruction is "in every place of worship I want men to pray with holy hands lifted up to God" (1 Timothy 2:8). How important is prayer? To fight the battle effectively, first, you pray, then second, get everybody else to pray.

Paul's letters are full of *his* prayers for those he's writing to, full of references to the continual time he spends praying for them, and full of requests that they take time to pray for *him*.

To the Colossian church he writes, "*Devote* yourselves to prayer… (4:2)" Devote is a pretty strong word. It is a word used quite often in the New Testament in relation to prayer and means "to occupy oneself diligently with something," "to pay persistent attention to," "to continually be in."

Prayer: to be occupied with it…diligently and continually. To pay attention to it…persistently. This picture is so different from prayers as an optional occasional add-on… nice but not necessary.

It was watching Jesus up close that finally triggered the disciples to ask him, "Please teach us to pray." They saw how devoted to prayer he was in the midst of incredible pressure and stress; diligently, persistently, continually.

Think of this statement from Luke: "the report of his power spread even faster, and vast crowds came to hear him preach and to be healed of their diseases. *But Jesus often withdrew to the wilderness for prayer*" (Luke 5:15–16, my emphasis).

Or this one: "One day soon afterward Jesus went up on a mountain to pray, and *he prayed to God all night*. At daybreak he called together all of his disciples and chose twelve of them to be apostles" (Luke 6:12–13, my emphasis).

Here is something I find interesting: there is no record in the Gospel accounts of the disciples doing any praying, let alone being devoted to prayer. In fact, at the end of three years with Jesus, we find them sleeping while Jesus is praying in the Garden of Gethsemane even though he's specifically asked them to pray (Luke 22:39–46). Yet in the accounts in Acts, they've made a huge transition. Over and over again we see them devoted to prayer—diligently, persistently, continually. Here are just a few examples. For the ten days between Jesus' ascension the powerful outpouring of the Holy Spirit at Pentecost, the disciples "all met together and were constantly united in prayer" (Acts 1:14). During that time when the issue of replacing Judas came up, they nominated two men, and then they all prayed" (Acts 1:24). Following Peter's first sermon when in response 3,000 put their faith in Jesus, were baptized, and "were added to the church that day" (Acts 2:41), what immediately characterized their lives? They "all...*devoted* themselves to the apostles' teaching, and to fellowship, and to sharing in meals (including the Lord's Supper), *and to prayer*" (Acts 2:42, my emphasis).

Here's just one more: when conflict arose over the distribution of food to help widows who'd become part of the believing community, the apostles gave this responsibility to seven others. They gave this as their reason, "Then we apostles can *spend our time in prayer* and teaching the word" (Acts 6:4, my emphasis).

What a transformation! They began with prayer a compartmentalized religious exercise. Even after lengthy exposure to Jesus—both watching his lived-out devotion to prayer and listening to his teaching about its incredible importance—they remained pretty prayerless. But as the responsibility for bringing God's Kingdom shifted from Jesus to them, they became genuinely *devoted* to prayer. And, as Paul's words in Colossians exemplifies, they called all believers to undergo that same transformation from prayer as occasional religious exercise (probably best left to special religious appointees) to prayer as an integrated part of our life: diligently, persistently, continually.

I have often encouraged myself by realizing how slow the disciples were on the uptake—even though they actually walked and talked with Jesus. But I've also struggled with actually following their steps of transformation. Prayer just has never—or at least rarely—been either "natural" or easy for me.

As I wrote at the beginning of this chapter, one insight has helped me greatly. It comes from two of Paul's statements:

1. "Epaphras, who is one of your number, a bond slave of Jesus Christ, sends you his greetings *always laboring earnestly* for you in his prayers" (Colossians 4:12–13, NASB, my emphasis).

2. "Now I urge you, brothers,…*to strive together with me in your prayers to God* for me" (Romans 15:30, NASB, my emphasis).

Taken together, here is the truth about what we are doing when we pray: we are *laboring*, the kind of labor that is *striving*. Simply put: Prayer is work—hard work.

That's become really encouraging to me, because it doesn't (except on very rare occasions) feel exhilarating or exciting or "flowing." It feels more like…work—and more often than not, *hard* work.

And there have been a number of helpful implications of prayer as work.

First, I thought that if prayer wasn't "fun" or easy, then that meant I wasn't cut out for it. But if prayer is work, then I need to view it as a responsibility I have as a follower of Jesus. What am I doing with that responsibility?

Second, work is a skill to be learned. For a number of years I was president of a start-up company in media and electronics. I had to develop skills in financial management, marketing, and manufacturing. I had to continually improve my skills in script-writing and photography. In fact, the list of skills and the necessity of continual improvement was never ending. So when I realized that prayer is work—*my* work—I immediately recognized that the work of prayer is a skill I shouldn't expect to be competent in to begin with. In fact, I should expect that I won't be able to do the work of prayer well at all to start with. But if I'm willing to learn—by doing and listening to those who have become skilled—I can continually do prayer better!

As I've gone about this skills learning, I've discovered that there are different prayer-work skills, all of which are related, but not the same. There are skills in different types of personal prayer. For example, there is prayer that develops intimacy with God, and prayer that is aimed at changing present circumstances. The skills for each are different. And those skills can (must!) be learned.

There are also skills in corporate prayer. What makes one meeting for corporate prayer more effective than another? The application of learned skills.

As I discovered by doing our prayer journeys to Spain, there are skills we need to learn to make praying outdoors in public as effective as possible.

The work of prayer requires learning the skills of prayer—and anyone can learn them, and keep learning them better—even me!

A third helpful application of the reality that prayer is work is this: how many of us get to our workplace, punch a time clock…but don't actually *work*? We're at our desk, or at our station, or at our job site. But we're simply *being present*, we're not actually *working*.

In the same way, how many times do we set aside time to pray, but when we get there, we don't really know what to say—so we say nothing? How many times do we go to a corporate prayer meeting, but then let others pray, and never say anything ourselves? Perhaps we feel that whatever we might try to say would sound pretty weak, even embarrassing. We're not sure what we can add to what others are praying. We get locked into saying nothing.

That's the time to remember the time clock. Ask yourself, "Do I want to just punch the time clock, or am I here to do work?" Let's face it, some workdays are more productive than others, and (going back to the skills issue) some people can do more work in a given time than others. But every one of us has been hired by God to do his work. And a vital part of his work is the work of prayer. So when I get to a place of prayer—either personally by myself, or in a corporate meeting—I've just determined I'm going to *work*, not just punch my time clock! And it's helped me a lot!

There is a fourth implication of realizing that prayer is work that has helped me understand the reality of pacing myself in prayer. In the same way I better not view my job—whether as president of a corporation or pastor of a local church—as a sprint, I need to view prayer as not a sprint, but a marathon. As a marathon, I can learn to pray with steadiness and "relaxed determination" knowing that I can wait for prayer to unfold as I—or we together—do the work of praying. I don't need to get to every subject today. I can arrange to focus on different things on different days. I can know in advance there will be downhill parts of the course—and uphill parts. If I need a water (or coffee) I have the time to take a drink. There's a whole lot of the work to go! And that drink can be physical—or it can be taking a spiritual drink by reading a passage of scripture, singing a worship song, anything that invites the Holy Spirit to give you fresh input. Prayer, like work, is not something to *get done*...it's something to *do*.

Now that I've described these four implications, I want to close this chapter by expanding our understanding of what it means that prayer is a skill—or set of skills—we can learn.

In the book by Malcolm Gladwell called *Outliers*, he takes a wide-ranging look at what makes people successful. One surprising discovery is what he called the "10,000 rule". To be really, really good at anything—playing the piano, playing soccer, writing incredible computer programs—requires that you spend 10,000 hours actually doing it—learning that particular skill. This rule held true for Bill Gates, who happened to be in perhaps the only place on earth where, as a young student, he had access to the new invention called a computer and could—and did—spend well over 10,000 hours learning the skills of programming.

The same rule held true for the Beatles, who took the world by storm in 1964, apparently an "overnight sensation." The truth is that by 1964 they had played together as a band for seven years, performing over 1200 times, including over 270 times in a single year in a string of clubs in Hamburg, Germany, averaging five hours per night. Their time learning their skills went far above the 10,000-hour rule!

Great pray-ers have spent hours learning great pray-er skills. They do the work of prayer well because they have spent the time required to learn to do it well. It's not simply because they "just have the gift of prayer...and I don't."

John Wimber, founder of the Vineyard movement, was used by God in the healing of thousands of people. But he saw his commission not to heal the sick, but to train every follower of Jesus to heal the sick. He often shared about letters he received from pastors who had attended one of his training conferences, had seen and experienced many people healed, then had returned home to discover "it doesn't work here...what's the deal?" John would respond "When you've prayed for two thousand people, write back and we can talk." His point was a version of the 10,000-hour rule: everything—including our use of the Holy Spirit's gifts—requires learning by doing.

The same is true of prayer.

Another recent book, *The Genius in All of Us*, by David Shenk, shares this discovery: none of us has a "talent scarcity." Instead, we have a "latent talent abundance." The limits each of us faces is "our inability to tap into what we already have. In other words, we need to "think of talent not as a thing, but as a process; not as something we have, but as something we do" (Reviewer Annie Murphy Paul, *New York Times Book Review*, March 21, 2010).

The ability to pray effectively, like any other sort of work, is abundantly potential in each of us. If we're willing to think of it as a process of development, we can *do it* in the confidence that we'll get better at it. Today. Tomorrow. By this time next year.

I have found tremendous encouragement and freedom in realizing that prayer is work—and work God intends all of us to do.

I believe you can too!

CHAPTER 4

Why Prayer?

Okay....Prayer may be work; but there is something illogical about prayer.

Didn't Jesus say, "Don't worry about these things, saying, 'What will we eat? What will we drink? What will we wear?' These things dominate the thoughts of unbelievers, but your heavenly father already knows all your needs" (Matthew 6:31–32)?

Extending that thought: If the Father knows and is concerned about things this small, he certainly knows and is concerned about "big" things as well. In fact, he must know and be concerned about absolutely everything. He's God!

To continue with Jesus' thought: Because this is so, "Seek first his kingdom and his righteousness, and all these things will be given to you as well" (Matthew 6:33, NIV).

What Jesus seems to be saying is "Don't pray about your personal needs (food, drink, clothing). Your Father knows what your needs are and doesn't need reminding. Get on about doing things he wants done (His kingdom things) and living rightly (his righteousness). As you do that, God will give you what he knows you need.

That, of course, is not what Jesus is saying at all. But there is a certain logic to this way of interpreting Jesus' words. What possible reason could there be for praying if God already knows what needs to be done, has purposes for everything, and is determined to and utterly capable of fulfilling all of them? The answer to the question "Why Prayer?" is really important if we are to become people who can pray in authentic faith and with the persistence the Bible recommends.

We have already seen that Jesus' words here in Matthew 6:31–33 are part of a much larger set of instructions. A few verses earlier Jesus without qualification says, "*When* [not if] you pray..." (Matthew 6:5). Along with giving and fasting, prayer is assumed to be a regular part of the normal Christian life. To be effective, it must be directed to God, not spoken aloud before others as a way to look good. But if our prayers are directed to the Father, *they will be heard and rewarded* (Matthew 6:6). And a bit further on, Jesus returns to the subject of praying saying, "Keep on asking...[because] your heavenly Father [will] give good gifts to those who ask him" (Matthew 7:7, 11).

Jesus says more about *how* to pray effectively—something practical worth exploring later—but at this moment we are considering the *why* of prayer. In particular, we are asking "If the Father already knows all needs (including ours), has long and deeply-held purposes, and is fully committed to and capable of fulfilling them, why pray?" We can just trust him to get it all done in his way and in his time.

To understand God's answer, let's begin by trying to better interpret Jesus' instructions not to worry about food, drink, and clothing, but instead to "seek the Kingdom of God above all else."

Just a few moments earlier, in his explanation of what to do when we pray, Jesus says, "Pray...this way: Our Father...Your Kingdom come, your will be done on earth as it is in heaven" (Matthew 6:9–10 NASB). What is the connection between *praying* "your Kingdom come" (Matthew 6:10), and "seek the Kingdom of God above all else" (Matthew 6:39)? Just this: A significant element of seeking the Kingdom is *praying* "Let your Kingdom come into this particular situation here on earth."

When Jesus instructs us to pray "Your Kingdom come," and "your will be done on earth," he is not saying two different things. The Kingdom of God is where God's rule as King is being implemented. It is where God's will is being carried out. God's will right now is being carried out in heaven. Jesus is telling us to ask that exactly the same thing be extended from heaven to earth. Therefore, to be people whose first priority is God's will not our needs, according to Jesus we must become people who spend time and energy on *asking God that his will be done here on earth.*

Why?

One of the most comprehensive of all Biblical revelations of human history is found in Psalm 2. Its placement among all the 150 Psalms highlights its significance. The first place in Psalms goes to the psalm which challenges each human being to choose God's way of living (his "law") or "the way of the wicked…sinner…and mockers." One leads to forever fruitfulness and the protection and care of God himself. The other leads to inevitable destruction. This first psalm makes sure we all understand that what we do and the choices we make to follow or not follow, to pay attention to or to disregard all that God reveals makes all the difference in how our lives actually turn out.

Having made the individually personal point, Psalm 2 gives us the opposite end of the human continuum: it gives us an overview of all history. And it uncovers the incredible importance of prayer. At the same time, it points to the answer to our question: Why Prayer?

The psalm begins with a satellite view of all the nations of the earth. Although this is a moment in time, it is clearly representative of *all* time. The description given is one that is true of any moment we might choose. It was true of the moment the psalm was written. It accurately summed up history to that moment. It is true at our moment of reading it today.

"Why are the nations so angry?

Why do they waste their time with futile plans?

The kings of the earth prepare for battle;

The rulers plot together against the Lord and against his anointed one.

'Let us break their chains,' they cry,

'And free ourselves from slavery to God.'"

The psalm's camera then zooms out beyond just the earthly view. God and heaven are now included in our picture.

"But the one who rules in heaven laughs,

The Lord scoffs at them.

Then in anger he rebukes them, terrifying them with his fierce fury.

For the Lord declares, 'I have placed my chosen king on the throne in Jerusalem on my holy mountain.'"

Remember, this psalm was first written and sung in the days of David. It would have expressed both the God-promised authority given to David to bring God's rule to Jerusalem and God's victory over the nations surrounding Israel, but also the God-revealed future hope. David was not the fulfilled *end* of God's purposes, but a *beginning*. The promise was of a Davidic descendant who would sit on David's throne, but whose reign would both last forever, and extend to all the nations of the earth (2 Samuel 7:11–16 and see e.g. Isaiah 49:5–7).

According to the Psalm's picture, where is God ruling? In heaven. And who is ruling on earth? Kings and rulers. To understand the *why* of prayer it is essential that we grasp this reality. We often confuse God's *sovereignty* (his ultimate authority over all things), with his *rule* (the active exercise of his authority).

Psalm 115:16 states: "The heavens belong to the Lord, *but he has given the earth to all humanity*" (my emphasis). The creation was made for us. God gave it to us—"Be fruitful and multiply. Fill the earth and govern it. Reign over [everything in it]" (Genesis 1:28). When we chose to reject God's rule over us, we were rejecting God's rule through us as his delegated agents over all the earth he gave to us. *And God did not take it back!*

This is not an arbitrary decision on God's part. It is the outcome and revelation of his character, which is unfailing love. In Hebrew, the word for "unfailing love" is *chesed*—a word which expresses both love and never-failing faithfulness together. Some time look up the word "love" in the Psalms. Over and over it describes God's unfailing love. It begins in Psalm 6:4 "Save me because of your unending love." Psalm 13:5 "But I trust in your unfailing love." Psalm 17:7 "Show the wonder of your great love." Psalm 21:7 "The unfailing love of the Most High." And, of course, the famous Psalm 23 "[your] love will follow me all the days of my life." The climax comes in Psalm 136 where one phrase repeats twenty-six times: "His love endures forever." This kind of love—unfailing love—is so essential to God's character that the apostle John says in one of his letters: "God is love…"—not *has* love, or *expresses* love, or *loves*…No. This is deeper, wider, much more essential.

The very nature of God *is* love.

Think of the implications!

The split between God's rule in heaven and God's rule on earth took place when Eve and then Adam chose to disobey God's instruction not to eat from "the tree of the knowledge of good and evil" (Genesis 2:17). In that moment, a question was posed—a question whose answer is unfolded in the Biblical revelation from Genesis on through to the end of Revelation. In fact, the unfolding of the answer is still taking place today.

The question posed by our rebellion was: God, if you are love, how can you restore your rule over those who have rejected your rule?

I'm not sure we've given much thought to the difficulty God faced—and still faces. Very simply, love cannot be forced, it can only be offered.

God's rule—the return of his active rule over the earth—cannot be gained by the exercise of God's *power*, but only by the *response* of those to whom this earth was given! It is only if we invite him to restore his rule can he do it.

This is why God's—and our—sworn enemy, Satan, believed he could deceive us, usurp the place of God over us, and never be defeated and deposed. Once we rejected God, we'd never be able to invite him back.

Perhaps you've had the painful experience of loving someone who didn't love you. I have, and more than once! But the experience that left the greatest mark in me was falling in love with a girl in my childhood. We saw each other each summer until my early teens, and every summer my love was renewed. What made it even more intense for me was never really knowing if she felt the same towards me as I felt towards her. I had other girlfriends through my teen years, but my heart always held out hope for my deepest love, although we had no contact with one another for a number of years.

There were a few significant twists in the story, but there came a time when we unexpectedly reconnected. I was sure God had brought us back together and all my hopes were rekindled. I finally invited her down for a weekend visit to the college I was attending. At dinner just before we parted I asked her to marry me. She responded, "When you invited me for this weekend, I knew you would ask me this question. I want to consider it before giving you an answer. I will let you know in the next two weeks."

The look in her eyes, the way she described how wonderful the weekend together had been the tone of her voice, all made a "yes" just a matter of a few more short days. And within a few days I received a letter in the mail. Eagerly I opened it and read her response: I respect and appreciate you. I think you're a great person, but I've decided to marry someone else.

Looking back now, I am so glad she said no. Just a couple of years later, I met the girl who won my heart and who has been my incredible partner in marriage, our family, and in ministry.

I'm glad for another reason. The pain of that experience developed in me an understanding of the limits of love's power and the pain of rejection. I could only invite the person I so loved to enter into love with me freely of her own choice. And that mirrors the truth of our relationship with God: He so loves us that he sent his Son as an invitation and through the cross a way back into a reciprocal love relationship.

Listen to Jesus—who carries the Father's heart: "O Jerusalem, Jerusalem, the city that kills the prophets and stones God's messengers! How often I have wanted [*longed*] to gather your children together as a hen protects her chicks beneath her wings, *but you wouldn't let me...*" Then as Luke describes it, "as he came closer to Jerusalem and saw the city ahead, he began to weep. "How I wish today that you...would understand the way of peace. But now it is too late..." (Luke 13:34 and 19:41–42, my emphasis).

This is no dispassionate discourse on Jerusalem's fate. It is the passion of a longing and broken heart. His love, God's love—is both the power of his mission—healing, expelling demons, cleansing lepers, proclaiming and bringing the kingdom rule of God—and the limit of his power—allowing rejection, submitting to suffering and ultimately the crucifixion.

What this means is that WITHOUT our prayer, God will NOT ACT. God *must* be invited to bring his rule because we *want* it. To repeat Psalm 115:16 "The heavens belong to the Lord, but he has given the earth to all humanity." He is waiting to be invited by those to whom he has given the authority and responsibility over this part of his creation.

Let's return to the unfolding picture in Psalm 2. After describing the rejection of the earth's kings and rulers, it reveals the response of God in heaven: he laughs.

Here is the crucial point. He doesn't laugh because he can so easily crush them with his infinitely greater power (for then there would be no one in the earth for him to love). He laughs because "I have placed my chosen king on the throne in Jerusalem" (Psalm 2:6). That is, God now has an *earthly ruler who wants God's rule of love restored to the earth.*

The Psalm continues from the king's perspective: "The king proclaims the Lord's decree: 'The Lord said to me, 'You are my son. Today I have become your Father. Only ask, and I will give you the nations as your inheritance, the whole earth as your possession'" (Psalm 2:7–8).

From our vantage point in history we know the king who is God's Son is Jesus Christ. He is fully human. He is the "second Adam". Indeed, Jesus is so fully human that Paul says the first Adam is "a symbol, a representation of Christ, who was yet to come." Yet to be God's king and God's Son is not enough! The Father says to His Son-King, *"Ask of me and I will give you the nations."* Without the Son's asking, God cannot respond—even though he *wants to*, has *planned to*, and has *promised he will*.

Nor could the Son ask *before* he humbled himself, taking on "the form of a slave and born as a human being" (Philippians 2:7). As the writer of Hebrews says, "Because God's children are human beings—made of flesh and blood—the Son also became flesh and blood…it was necessary for him to be made in every aspect like us" (Hebrews 2:14, 17). He could only ask *as a man*.

Do you begin to see how and why prayer is so crucial? How much authority rests on those who pray—or choose not to ask? It has nothing to do with *feeling* like praying. It has simply to do with wanting to see God's love and power released into earth's realities that need the change his rule would bring.

"So pray this way: Our Father in heaven, blessed be your name. May your Kingdom come [right here and right now]. May your will be done on earth as it is in heaven…" We, to whom you have given the authority and responsibility for the earth, are the ones extending this invitation. We are asking for your rule of love to be restored in, through, and around us now. In the name of your Son, our great savior and king, Jesus.

CHAPTER 5

Where Should We Pray?

This is not a trick question.

On the one hand, Jesus clearly tells us: "When you pray, go away by yourself, shut the door behind you, and pray to your Father in private" (Matthew 6:6). Yet everywhere in scripture there are examples of public, not behind-the-door-away-by-yourself prayer. And I don't mean public prayer in the church service. I mean public prayer right out in the open.

Is Jesus contradicting these other examples? Is he superseding them: "that was then, but this is now?" I don't think so! He himself often prayed in public. In the very same public place where he called out to the crowd, "Come to me, all of you who are weary and heavy laden," he prays out loud, "O Father, Lord of heaven and earth, thank you for hiding these things from those who think themselves wise and clever, and for revealing them to the childlike" (Matthew 11:28, 25). When he is about to feed 5,000 men, plus women and children, with five loaves of bread and two fish, he first "took the fives loaves and two fish, looked up toward heaven, and blessed them" (Matthew 14:19). Standing directly in front of the tomb where Lazarus' corpse has been laid out, Jesus orders people to roll the stone covering the tomb's mouth aside…"Then Jesus looked up to heaven and said, 'Father, thank you for hearing me. You always hear me, but I said it out loud for the sake of all these people standing here…'" (John 11:41, 42).

So why does Jesus apparently contradict both scripture and himself when he tells us to pray in private? The point Jesus is making here in Matthew chapter 6—not only about prayer, but also about giving and fasting—is that we do it for God, not to gain the admiration of other people. He is addressing the *purpose* for which we pray, not a prescribed and proscribed place to pray.

In this chapter I want to make the case that we are authorized to, and need to, engage in public prayer—prayer in public places.

Earlier, I shared that my wife, Nancy, and I were asked to take the lead in encouraging a partnership of churches to pray for Spain. One of the most impactful things we did was to bring groups of people from these churches to Spain in order to pray "on site with insight." In the first few years, when we had very few contacts in Spain, we traveled from city to city, rooming as close to the city center as possible, and spending a couple of hours in the morning and evening worshipping with a guitar, and praying for that particular city and for the nation. Although we often gathered indoors at the start of the day for some teaching, sharing and personal ministry, our worship and prayer took place in public plazas and parks.

We have also done this in the community surrounding our church here in the U.S. I want to encourage others to do this with the conviction that God actually calls us to do this!

Perhaps you have heard someone say that when you want to research a particular topic in the Bible, an important place to start is where that topic is first raised. This is sometimes called "The Law of First Mention" or "The Place of Primary Reference." If we understand that prayer is a directed communication between us and God, prayer's passage of primary reference is…Genesis 3!

"When the cool evening breezes were blowing, the man and his wife heard the Lord God walking about in the garden. So they hid from the Lord God among the trees. Then the Lord God called to the man, 'where are you?'" (Genesis 3:8-9).

This was clearly a regular, daily experience. It was in *community*, (Adam and Eve together) and *in public* (in the open). It also describes prayer as 2-way communication. You might be thinking, "Of course it was in public—it was in the Garden of Eden." But it is at least worth taking note that the very first recorded experience of prayer is in community and in public. Let's follow the Bible's unfolding story of prayer.

The second recorded prayer experience is in Genesis 4:

"When it was time for the harvest, Cain presented some of his crops as a gift to the Lord. Abel also brought a gift—the best of the first-born lambs from his flock. The Lord accepted Abel and his gift, but did not accept Cain and his gift. This made Cain very angry, and he looked dejected. "Why are you so angry?" the Lord asked Cain."

Again, there is 2-way communication, and it takes place out in the open, in public.

Let's fast-forward to the beginning of the salvation story. Abraham, after winning a battle against a neighboring king and recovering all that had been plundered, meets the king of Sodom and a mysterious figure, Melchizedek. In the Psalms, God reveals to David that a king will come whose rule will extend out "over the whole earth." About this one, God says, I have taken an oath: "You are a priest forever in the order of Melchizedek" (Psalm 110:6, 4).

Throughout Israel's history, no king could serve as priest—nor could any priest serve as king. Yet Melchizedek is both "King of Salem and a priest of God" (Genesis 14:18). As Scripture's story unfolds, as the writer of Hebrews states, Melchizedek turns out to be "a priest…resembling the Son of God." He appears to Abraham as a representative of Jesus Christ, himself. And to fully validate this symbolic correspondence, the king-priest brings Abraham "some bread and wine". This anticipates God's salvation promise fulfilled in Jesus Christ. He is the one who offers all of Abraham's descendants by faith the bread of his own body broken for us and the wine of his own blood poured out for us. Then the king-priest blesses Abraham, while Abraham gives him "a tenth of all the goods he had recovered."

It is hard to imagine a more significant prayer event—one whose implications span the whole of salvation history. Where does it occur? In public, before the eyes of the King of Sodom, all his people who'd been taken captive then set free, and his allies—the kings Aner, Eshcol, and Mamre—along with all their people. It takes place in public in the presence of both believers—Abraham and his few hundred followers (Genesis 14:14)—and unbelievers—the four kings with their few thousand people.

Consider two other highly significant prayer events in the Old Testament:

> "At the usual time for offering the evening sacrifice, Elijah the prophet walked up to the altar and prayed, 'O Lord, God of Abraham, Isaac, and Jacob, prove today that you are God in Israel and that I am your servant. Prove that *I have done this at your command.* O Lord, answer me! Answer me so these people will know that you, O Lord, are God and that you have brought them back to yourself.'
>
> Immediately the fire of the Lord flashed down from heaven and burned up the young bull, the wood, the stones, and the dust. It even licked up all the water in the trench! And when all the people saw it, they fell face down on the ground and cried out, "The Lord— he is God! Yes, the Lord is God!"
>
> 1 Kings 18:36–39, my emphasis

This is the climax of a familiar story. Ahab, king of Northern Israel, and his queen, Jezebel, have conspired to wipe out every prophet who worships and speaks for God. In their place they have established the worship of Baal, a Canaanite deity, with its own coterie of cultic prophets. For three and half years, God's premier prophet, Elijah, was in hiding, and during that time there was no rain.

Finally, at God's command, Elijah emerges from hiding and challenges the prophets of Baal to a contest: each of us will call on our god to consume the sacrifice prepared with fire from heaven. After hours of public prayer with no response to the prayers of Baal's prophets, the Old Testament narrative describes Elijah's public prayer and God's public response—fire so intense it consumes not only the sacrificial bull, but the wood, the stones, the dust and the water filling the trench around the altar.

The phrase "I have done all this at your command" is important for more than one reason. But here, it reinforces the significance of *public* prayer in the presence of both believers and unbelievers. It is not that *all* prayers must be public. It is that some prayer should be public. This is not simply *our* idea, but *God's* directive.

One final instructive Old Testament example is from the life of Daniel. He was neither a priest nor a prophet. Instead, he was an immigrant (by forced exile) in an unbelieving nation and served in its government. He is a representative of the sort of vocational life most of us as Christians lead: we work in and for and are paid by businesses, educational institutions, or government agencies in the world system, not the church. Daniel not only worked there, he was highly successful and respected there. And he was a public witness to God everywhere he served. He was also devoted to prayer. On more than one occasion, that witness got him in trouble.

Knowing Daniel's habits of personal prayer, a group of colleagues, jealous of his power and favor with the king, proposed an executive order:

> "So the administrators and high officers went to the king and said, 'Long live King Darius! We are all in agreement—we administrators, officials, high officers, advisors, and governors—that the king should make a law that will be strictly enforced. Give orders that for the next thirty days any person who prays to anyone, divine or human—except to you, your Majesty—will be thrown into the den of lions. And now your Majesty, issue and sign this law so it cannot be changed, an official law of the Medes and Persians that cannot be revoked.' So King Darius signed the law."
>
> Daniel 6:6–9

If there were ever a good time to take a break from praying for a few days, this was it. Or if not a full break, certainly making sure that it only happened after going away by yourself, shutting the door behind you, and praying to your Father in private (remember Jesus in Matthew 6:6?). Here is how Daniel responded:

> "But when Daniel learned that the law had been signed, he went home and knelt down *as usual* in his upstairs room, *with its windows open to Jerusalem.* He prayed three times a day, *just as he had always done,* giving thanks to his God. Then the officials went together to Daniel's house and found him praying and asking for God's help."
>
> Daniel 6:10–11, my emphasis

We know the rest of the story. Daniel was taken into custody, thrown overnight into a den of hungry lions, and was protected, set free and restored to an even higher position of authority than before. In the aftermath of the miraculous deliverance, the king issued a nationwide proclamation that "the God of Daniel…is the living God…[who] will endure forever…[whose] kingdom will never be destroyed…and [whose] rule will never end" (Daniel 6:26).

At the heart of this story is Daniel's habitual, well-known *public* prayer. It simply reaffirms the evidence of the entire Old Testament: prayer in public is God-directed and endorsed, and is intended to be a living witness to believers and unbelievers alike. It demonstrates that our God is worthy of our worship. It demonstrates that we believe he hears our prayers. It demonstrates that he is Ruler over all the earth: every street and city, every community and nation.

This attitude towards public prayer is displayed throughout the New Testament as well. For example, when Paul and his small missionary team first left Asia Minor and, in response to a supernatural vision, traveled to Europe, then entered Philippi, "a major city of that district of Macedonia" (Acts 16:12). On the first Sabbath, they went to a site along the river where they thought any Jewish people in the area might gather for prayer.

What that means is that meeting for public prayer on the Sabbath was a normal part of Jewish life across the Roman Empire.

But the story continues. Paul and his team find a group of people as expected. They share the message of Jesus. One of the leading women, Lydia, becomes the first to believe, and she and other members of her household are the first to be baptized. Now, more and more people begin coming "to the place of prayer"—to pray and worship and listen to Paul's teaching. One day as Paul is walking to the meeting place, he expels a demonic spirit from a woman fortune-teller. The men who own her as a slave and who have been making money from her fortune-telling are furious. They have Paul and Silas arrested, convicted, beaten severely and thrown into prison. They are placed in the inner dungeon and have their feet clamped in stocks. Luke, a part of the team, describes what happened next:

> "Around midnight Paul and Silas were *praying and singing hymns* to God, and the other prisoners were listening."
>
> Acts 16:25, my emphasis

They engage in *public prayer* before unbelievers.

They experience a *public result* from their witness:

> "Suddenly, there was a massive earthquake, and the prison was shaken to its foundations. All the doors immediately flew open, and the chains of every prisoner flew off!"
>
> Acts 16:26

The effect on the jailer was to fall trembling at their feet and ask, "Sirs, what must I do to be saved?" (Acts 16:30).

Public prayer gains for God a public witness to his public presence. It also creates a place for him to reveal his power to those who will never enter a church building or a private meeting.

The aspect of prayer I am focusing on in this book is distinct from praying for individual people for healing or other similar needs. It's important to note that this principle of prayer in public certainly extends to prayer for individuals. We need to take all types of prayer out into the public. God wants to display himself—and we are his chosen witnesses.

To all of these examples—and the Bible is filled with others too many to count—Paul adds a direct command from God to the Church. It is found in his first letter to Timothy, assigned to pastor and lead the fledgling church in Ephesus:

> "This *command* I entrust to you, Timothy, my son, in accordance with the prophecies previously made concerning you, that by them you fight the good fight…"
>
> 1 Timothy 1:18, NASB, my emphasis

Paul is telling Timothy that he has a *command* for him to follow and live out. It is a command that will enable him to *fight the good fight*. There have been some prophetic words spoken to Timothy regarding his gifting and calling to be a pastor/leader. This command which Paul is about to give will enable him in his role and responsibility as pastor/leader to fight effectively.

What is the fight? It is the great battle between the only two kingdoms: God's Kingdom and the kingdom of darkness. It is a battle for the faith of men and women. Paul will describe its outline after he gives Timothy the content of the command:

> "I urge you, first of all, to pray for all people. Ask God to help them, intercede on their behalf…"
>
> 1 Timothy 2:1

The command that will enable us to fight this great battle is *first of all to pray*. By all means, we must proclaim. We certainly must share the good news. But first of all, *we must pray*. Timothy can't save anyone. I can't, nor can you. Only God can save. As the Psalm says, "Unless the Lord builds a house, the work of the builders is wasted" (Psalm 127:1). Prayer is our invitation (as outlined in the previous chapter) to God for his intervention in our sphere of responsibility.

The result of our prayer, according to Paul, will affect the lives of those for whom we pray, including "kings and all who are in authority" (as argued in chapter 4). Our prayer will allow God to get the message through to people (through our personal sharing, something he so intensely wants to do, because he "wants everyone to be saved and to understand the truth" (1 Timothy 2:4).

Paul then summarizes the message that brings the fight into enemy territory. It is the "message about faith and truth" that "God gave to the world at just the right time." It is this message: "there is only one God and one Mediator who can reconcile God and humanity—the man Christ Jesus. He gave his life to purchase freedom for everyone" (1 Timothy 2:5–7).

Then Paul adds a final, practical element: "Therefore…" (1 Timothy 2:8). The command is to pray so that God can enable our sharing of his message to be effective: allowing people who hear to experience saving faith and an understanding of the truth.

Therefore, in order to effectively carry out this fight-empowering command:

> "I want the men in every place to pray, lifting up holy hands, without wrath and dissension."
>
> 1 Timothy 2:8, NASB

The New Living Translation, which I have chosen to use throughout this book as my default text, inserts this phrase, "in every place of worship." The words "of worship" do not appear in the underlying Greek text, and I believe they give a somewhat misleading connotation to Paul's words. I prefer the wording of the NASB (the NIV uses "everywhere" which is similarly unrestricted): "in every place." The evidence we have looked at throughout the rest of scripture does not limit "every place" to "inside church walls" or "inside places of worship." Instead, it expands "every place" to include every *public* place. This command to pray includes the instruction to take prayer *for* the streets *to* the streets. God will be as public as we are willing to make him. And the public witness of *prayer* is a living demonstration of how the people of God relate to God—our Father, Creator, Maker of Heaven and earth, Savior, Redeemer, our Loving King to whom belongs all authority in all the earth—"*every place.*"

Isn't this where all of history is going? According to the vision/experience given to John the Apostle, first the twenty-four elders respond as Jesus, the Lion/Lamb, is found worthy to take the scroll, representing the Title Deed to this world. They sing "a new song" celebrating the Lamb who was slain. Then John "looks again" and hears "the voices of thousands and millions of angels around the throne singing "Worthy is the Lamb." The story and the vision have not yet reached their climax. The story and the vision are flowing towards something so incredible, so breathtaking, so encompassing that John can hardly comprehend what he sees. *"And then I heard every creature in heaven and on earth and under the earth and in the sea."* They sang:

> "Blessing and honor and glory and power belong the one sitting on the throne and to the Lamb forever and ever".
>
> Revelation 5:1–13, selected, my emphasis

Where is this greatest of all worship and prayer meetings taking place? Everywhere…in every place…in public.

Let's already participate in what is not yet fulfilled—but will be!

CHAPTER 6

Our Prayer and The Helper

One of the most astonishing things Jesus ever said was this: "I tell you the truth, of all who have ever lived, none is greater than John the Baptist. Yet even the least person in the Kingdom of Heaven is greater than he" (Matthew 11:11).

What does he mean? And what does this mean for us as pray-ers?

Jesus clearly explains the first half of his statement by saying that John is far greater than any prophet because he is the "messenger" sent to "prepare [the] way" for God's Messiah, the very Son of God. Prophets themselves were especially great among all other people because they were direct recipients of God's own words. What made John so much greater was that he was preparing the people of God for the coming of the Living Word—Jesus himself—and the long-promised Kingdom of God. But there's more to it—and more which will help us understand the second half of Jesus' statement—the half he did not explain so clearly.

In Numbers, there is a story which reveals something essential to every prophet. Moses has begged God for help in "carrying" all of Israel—"a load far too heavy" for him to carry alone (Numbers 11:14). So at God's instruction, Moses gathers seventy elders and stations them around the Tabernacle. Here's what happened:

> "And the Lord came down in the cloud and spoke to Moses. Then He gave the seventy elders the same Spirit that was on Moses. And when the Spirit rested upon them, they prophesied."
>
> Numbers 24b–25b

The source of any prophecy is the Holy Spirit. The greatness of any prophet comes from the greatness of the Person who rests upon them.

What is "so much greater" about the Messiah according to John, His messenger? It is (among other things) that "he will *baptize* you with the Holy Spirit" (Matthew 3:11, my emphasis). The greatness of every prophet lies in the fact that the Holy Spirit rests on him or her. The *greatness* of John lies in the fact that the Holy Spirit resting on him is making a way in people's hearts to receive the One who will *give the Spirit to all.*

This, by the way, fulfills the prophetic prayer of Moses in the story we just recounted; "I wish that all the Lord's people were prophets and that the Lord would put his Spirit upon them all!" (Numbers 11:29). This prayer reveals the heart—and plan—of God, and is the first of many times this promise of the Holy Spirit given to all is reiterated throughout the Old Testament. The most well-known of these reiterations is found in Joel 2:28 "Then, after doing all those things, I will pour out my Spirit upon all people. *Your sons and daughters will prophesy...*In those days I will pour out my Spirit even on servants—men and women alike..."

And when Peter stands up to address the crowd following the coming of the Holy Spirit at Pentecost, he quotes that scripture and says, what you see and hear us experiencing is what God promised through Joel—and God is offering this to you, too!

Indeed, this gift of the Holy Spirit is so significant that Jesus calls it "*the* gift the Father promised" (Acts 1:4, NIV, my emphasis), and Peter cites it as the certain proof that Jesus was raised from the dead and has been "exalted to the place of highest honor in heaven, at God's right hand." Here is the certain proof: "And the Father, *as he had promised*, gave him the Holy Spirit to pour out on us, just as you see and hear today" (Acts 2:3-33, my emphasis).

Therefore, to return to Jesus' statement in Matthew 11:11, "even the least person in the Kingdom of Heaven is greater than" John the Baptist because even the least is meant to receive the Holy Spirit. The Holy Spirit is no longer given to a select few individuals for limited times and restricted tasks. Now, the gift is to be poured out on all.

One of the practical results of receiving the Holy Spirit is as a supernatural partner with each of us in praying. But praying in partnership with Him is not automatic. Look at these two descriptions—one from

Revelation, one from Ephesians. First, pay attention to how John describes what he was doing when Jesus appeared to him:

> "I, John, am your brother and your partner...[that is, I am not greater than any of you—I am like you...I am your brother and your partner]. I was exiled to the island of Patmos for preaching the word of God and for my testimony about Jesus. It was the Lord's Day, and I was worshipping in the Spirit."
>
> Revelation 1:9–10

In the original Greek text, the words John wrote do not contain the word "worshipping." He simply states: "I was in the Spirit." The reason the translators add the word "worshipping" is because the clear sense of John's description is that he was communicating with God in prayer—whether praising, thanking, or interceding and asking is not clear. What he does make clear is that he was communicating "in the Spirit." Another way of saying that is: "in intimate partnership with the Holy Spirit."

In the Ephesians passage, Paul uses the same language:

> "A final word: be strong in the Lord and in his mighty power...We are not fighting against flesh-and-blood enemies, but against evil rulers and authorities of the unseen world...*Pray in the Spirit* at all times and on every occasion. Stay alert and be persistent in your prayers..."
>
> Ephesians 6:10, 12, 18 my emphasis

What Paul is reminding all of us about is that in becoming Jesus' disciples, we have switched sides in the great battle of two kingdoms—God's and Satan's. The battle is one being fought, as he describes in his second letter to the church in Corinth, "not with weapons of the flesh" but with weapons that have "divine power" (2 Corinthians 10:3–4, NASB). And one of the ways we engage in this battle is by praying—"at all times and on every occasion."

That is, prayer is not a last resort nor an infrequent exercise. To be effectively engaged in the battle that is going on everywhere, every day, relentlessly, we must be on the alert, praying persistently.

But notice, *how* does Paul say we need to pray? He says, "Pray in the Spirit." It is what John was doing. It is praying in an intimate partnership with the Holy Spirit.

There is a wonderful description of how God intends this to work in practice contained in a prophecy of Isaiah. It first encourages us as God's people to come to him in prayer, because although he *wants* to, he can't act until we ask:

> "So the Lord must wait for you to come to him so he can show you his love and compassion...He will be gracious if you ask for help. He will surely respond to the sound of your cries."

What could more clearly invite us to pray "at all time and on every occasion"? But the practical instruction about praying in partnership with the Holy Spirit follows:

> "You will see your teacher with your own eyes. Your own ears will hear him".
>
> Isaiah 30:20b

To understand what the Lord is about to reveal, we need to first understand how the promise of "the teacher" is fulfilled. In the first place, "the teacher" is referring to Jesus, whom God's people would (incredibly!) see with their own eyes and hear with their own ears. But that is not all God has in mind! Jesus began the fulfillment when he took on our form and lived among us. The fulfillment does not, however, end with his departure. Instead, as he told his disciples "in fact, it is best for you that I go away, [because then] I will send [the Advocate] to you...the Spirit of Truth...[who] will guide you into all truth...He will bring me glory by telling you whatever he receives from me" (John 16:7, 13–14).

The practical interaction between each follower of Jesus and Jesus the teacher did not stop at his ascension. In fact, it was enhanced and extended to every follower wherever they may be and all the time. The Holy Spirit is right now continuing to fulfill God's promise to his people as revealed through Isaiah.

> "Whether you turn to the right or to the left, you will hear a voice behind you, saying, 'This is the way; walk in it.'"
>
> Isaiah 30:21, NIV

Have you ever said this to God: "Just tell me what to do and I'll do it?" God has a different plan: "Seek my way by taking some steps—with eyes and ears alert and open to see and hear my 'yes', or to note its absence!" This way of doing things encourages us to be aggressive in our faith instead of passive.

It also reveals God's practical strategy for effective pray-ers. Instead of trying to figure out in advance what God wants us to pray about, and what his will is for that situation so that we can pray in tune with whatever that is, God reveals a different strategy: just start praying! But be alert to sensing God's "Yes"—or the emptiness of his "Not exactly."

Jack Hayford once talked about having a "Butterfly Anointing." Butterflies flutter this way and that way. He used that as a good picture of how his mind often works when he prays. "Where am I going with this thought? What am I doing? Will I land on anything I'm supposed to? Will this accomplish anything?" But without fluttering and landing here, and then there, we'll never "hear a voice *behind* us saying, 'Yes! This is the way…Now walk in it."

Do you see how wonderfully practical a strategy that gives us for becoming effective pray-ers?

Our first task is to start praying.

Then, as we are praying, we need to be listening for "a voice behind us." What this means is this. As we pray, there will be a sense of "*this* is the right focus." Sometimes that sense will be accompanied by a picture of something, or by a particular scripture verse, sometimes by a scripture reference which needs to be looked up (having a Bible handy is a good idea), sometimes by a word or a phrase. Then what is crucial is to take hold of that revelation and begin praying in accordance with it.

It is just at this point that I have seen many people abort what the Holy Spirit is partnering with us to do. Instead of using the revelation as a springboard for prayer, or a pathway to pray along, they take the revelation as the *goal*. If in a group, they will excitedly share what they saw or heard as though that is the end of praying. Instead, we need to receive that revelation as the Holy Spirit giving us direction about how to start praying with faith and confidence. Instead of seeing the revelation as the goal, we must see it as what it really is: the Coach sending in the play.

To pray "seeing and listening" is a very different way of learning to pray than just praying. One is seeking to work with our Partner. The other is doing it all on our own.

This New Covenant God has made with us is the promise not only of forgiveness through the blood of Jesus, but of the gift of the Holy Spirit. For example, in the opening paragraph of Paul's letter to the Ephesians he writes: "And when you believed in Christ, he identified you as his own by giving you the Holy Spirit, whom he promised long ago" (Ephesians 1:13b). This gift is at the very center of Peter's offer of salvation in the very first evangelistic sermon ever preached: "Each of you must repent of your sins and turn to God, and be baptized in the name of Jesus Christ for the *forgiveness of your sins*. Then you will receive *the gift of the Holy Spirit*. This promise is to you, and to your children, and even to the Gentiles—all who have been called by the Lord our God" (Acts 2:38-39, my emphasis).

I am pressing this because we need to get hold of how essential this is to the normal Christian life. "Hearing a voice behind you," is not a rare and special experience for rare and special people. It is the way life as a Christian is meant to be lived. But because many of us have not been taught to expect this, we've not learned the practical skills of being alert to see, hear, and then act on what our partner, the Holy Spirit, is revealing.

John Wimber, founder of the Vineyard, and Henry Blackaby, the tremendously influential Baptist who produced the "Experience God" training program, emphasized the way Jesus carried out his ministry. Jesus described this himself in John 5:19—"the Son can do nothing by himself. He does only what he sees the Father doing." We could easily assume this means that Jesus saw well in advance "what the Father was doing." The more natural reality is that Jesus went about his life focused on announcing, explaining, and doing the works of the inbreaking Kingdom of God. As he did, he was intentionally alert to see and hear where God was at work. When he recognized "God working," then he focused on doing/partnering with that.

Certainly, there were many things that the Holy Spirit revealed to Jesus in advance—most certainly his suffering, death, and resurrection on the third day. But there are many other events in the course of his ministry that surprised him: the incredible unbelief in his home town of Nazareth, the equally incredible faith of the Roman Centurion asking for Jesus to heal his servant "with just a word," the woman in the crowd who touched his robe with such faith that "power flowed out of him" and healed her. "Who touched me?" Jesus asked.

Now consider these three stories:

First, there is the story of Jesus healing a paralyzed man at a large pool of water called Bethesda. There were dozens of other sick or severely handicapped people also there. Yet Jesus singled out that one man and healed him. Why? Although John, in recounting this story, doesn't tell us, the clear implication is that as Jesus was passing by, he "saw" the "Father working" on that particular man. To put it another way, Jesus was paying attention to the Holy Spirit communicating in some way *"this* is the way… walk in it." This might be the sense of "light" on a person. It could be sensing what is wrong with a person—and understanding that God is revealing it not so Jesus can know it, but because God wants Jesus to *act* on that knowledge and to heal him. In this instance, the Holy Spirit not only revealed what needed to be healed physically, but the connection between the man's physical condition and some area of sin in his life. We know this because after Jesus has healed him and sent him on his way, he finds him a second time and warns him to "stop sinning, or something even worse may happen to you" (John 5:14).

This particular event leads directly to an argument with the religious leaders. They were upset because Jesus had commanded the healed man to pick up and carry the mat he had been laying on. This violated their laws regulating the Sabbath. Jesus response is, "My Father is always working, and so am I…the Son can do nothing by himself. He only does what he sees the Father doing" (John 5:17, 19).

The healing event is directly tied to Jesus' statement about doing what he sees the Father doing. Why? I believe John is describing an example of "doing what he sees the Father doing."

This becomes even clearer when compared with the next two stories. They come from the lives of disciples whom Jesus trained to do what he did.

In the very first days following the coming of the Holy Spirit at Pentecost, Peter and John are walking up to the gate of the Temple when a man lame from birth begs them to take pity on him and give him a few coins. Luke, who is writing the account, tells us that the man has been placed there "each day", presumably for many years. How many times might Jesus have seen him? Certainly Peter and John had often seen him because this was not the first time they had gone in and out of the Temple gate where the man was placed each day.

On *this* day, when the man asked them for money, Luke says, "Peter and John looked at him intently." Then they spoke those now-famous words: "Silver and gold have I none. But in the name of Jesus Christ of Nazareth, rise up and walk" (Acts 3:6, KJV).

Healing the man on that particular day has everything to do with "looking at him intently." Peter and John had watched, listened, and learned as Jesus "did what he saw the Father doing." He got up and often went off for a while to pray by himself. He ate breakfast. He walked with his disciples to the next place on his mission to proclaim the inbreaking presence of the Kingdom of God, healing the sick and casting out demons. And along the way, he was continually alert to being directed by the Holy Spirit: focus on this particular person, stay in this place—or move on from this place even though there is much success here. Jesus was living out—and modeling and training his disciples to live out a partnership with the Holy Spirit.

The third story, also told by Luke, is even clearer:

> "While they were at Lystra, Paul and Barnabas came upon a man with crippled feet. He had been that way from birth, so he had never walked. He was sitting and listening as Paul preached. Looking straight at him, Paul realized he had faith to be healed. So Paul called to him in a loud voice, 'Stand up!' And the man jumped to his feet and started walking."
>
> Acts 14:8–10

Paul is going about his business. But as he is preaching, he notices something about a man who is sitting in the listening crowd. Why does he notice this particular man? Because Paul is doing what Jesus did: he is being alert to impressions communicated by the Holy Spirit. What Paul notices is some sort of indication given to him by the Holy Spirit. Whatever it was, Paul responded first by "looking straight at him." He focused his attention where the Holy Spirit was indicating the Father's attention was focused. As he did that, the Holy Spirit revealed—again, Paul is experiencing a *knowing sense*—that this man had faith to be healed.

The truth is that each of us as followers of Jesus are intended and designed to operate as partners with the Holy Spirit in this same way—both as we go about our daily lives as in these Biblical accounts, and as we pray.

Cindy Jacobs tells the story of learning to pay attention to impressions given by the Holy Spirit and responding in prayer in her book, *Possessing The Gates of The Enemy*:

> "At 2:00am I awakened with a start. The indicators were familiar: I felt a sense of danger and agitation. Deep within I began to pray, *God what is wrong? Is someone in trouble?* Almost instantly I saw a mental picture or vision of good friends Dave and Cheryl Barton. They were driving their van from the Dallas area where they lived to our meeting with their three children curled up asleep in the back. All of a sudden, in the vision, the van's right front wheel rolled off, and the van careened wildly into a horrible accident.
>
> I knew immediately that they were in serious danger and that God wanted me to pray that the wheel bearings would hold until we could contact the Barton's and warn them...The hours dragged on as I cried out to God to keep that wheel in place and protect them. All through the night I sensed a tremendous battle taking place in the heavenlies.
>
> The next day I hounded the registration desk until finally a call came into the room. They had arrived. I ran to their room and pounced on them. "Are you all right? Has anything happened to the van?" Between hugs they said that everything was just fine. After I told them about my night of prayer, Cheryl mentioned that she had heard a funny sound in the van the night before, but Dave had not noticed it. I urged them strongly to check the right ball bearings. Dave and Cheryl know me well enough to know that I would

not say this lightly; so before Dave took the van on the road again, he and Mike drove it to a garage.

When they finally returned to the hotel they were grinning from ear to ear. Mike had a little bag in his hand. "The trophies of intercession," he said. It held the bearings from the right front wheel.

As we heard their story we marveled at God's mercy and care for the Barton family. The mechanic took off the left wheel bearings first and exclaimed, "I don't see how you could have driven this without having it seize up on you." After checking the right wheel he was really amazed: "This one is worse than the other!" He said that there was no way they should have been able to drive without having the wheels come off. He went on to explain that the spindle, which should have been totally ruined, was not damaged.

Dave grinned and told us, "We couldn't let an opportunity to share about the Lord pass by, and so I said, 'Do you know why we came in to have our wheels checked?'" For the next half hour the men witnessed to an astonished mechanic and I thanked God in my heart for waking me to pray."

Not every signal from our Helper, the Holy Spirit, is as dramatic—nor are the results of our prayer so immediate and known. But they are an encouragement to be alert to God's voice—often whispered—behind us and to pray in faith for results we may only know of in heaven.

In my experience, there are people who find it easier to learn to do this, and others who find it harder. We seem to be wired differently in this as in every other dimension of our lives. Some of us find building relationships is easier; some find that harder. Some of us find sharing our faith easier; some find that harder. But God clearly invites and expects all of us to learn how to share our faith, to build relationships, and to be alert to the promptings of the Holy Spirit. All of us can learn!

Let me conclude this chapter by applying this to praying with others. So often group prayer is really solo prayer in which pray-ers happen to be in the same room. One prays for our school, another prays for their neighbor who is sick with pneumonia, someone else prays for an upcoming outreach event. This is like ripping open a shotgun shell and then firing each individual piece of buckshot one at a time at a different target.

The power of a shotgun is that it focuses all the buckshot at a single target. Each piece strikes at a slightly different point from a slightly different angle—but all are grouped in one circumscribed location.

That is analogous to focusing many individual prayers at the same target. While one prayer will have some effect, combining a number of prayers will access much greater power.

Why did Jesus say:

> "If two or you agree here on earth concerning anything you ask, my Father in heaven will do it for you. For where two or three gather together in my name, I am there among them."
>
> Matthew 18:19–20

Does he mean that when we are alone, he is not with us? That is certainly not true! Scripture, and the living experience of believers throughout history, speak of and celebrate the God who knows and is with us personally. As the prophet Hanani told King Asa in a time of intense crisis, "The eyes of the Lord search the whole earth in order to strengthen those whose hearts are fully committed to him" (2 Chronicles 16:9).

Think of the long line of Biblical heroes who experienced God's presence while they were alone: Abraham most profoundly when God makes his covenant with him in Genesis 15; Moses at the burning bush and forty years later at Mt. Sinai, but also daily when Moses encountered him in the special Tent of Meeting (Exodus 33:7–11); Elijah outside the cave on Mt. Sinai (1 Kings 19:8–18). You get the picture!

And then we come to Jesus who often got up early or sent the disciples away late so that he could be alone to pray (e.g., Matthew 14:23). In fact, the very end of the Bible is a recounting of God's presence with John while alone, in exile on the island of Patmos.

Why, then, does Jesus talk about being present when a group of believers get together to pray? I believe Jesus is describing a practical strategy for *intensification*. Throughout scripture there is a consistent theme pointing to an intensification of authority, which has a powerful application to becoming effective in our praying.

For example, whenever a person is accused of wrongdoing in God's community of Israel, judgment may be rendered only if there are at least "two or three witnesses" (Deuteronomy 17:6 and 19:15). Both Jesus and Paul reiterate this for God's new community, the Church, in Matthew 18:16 and 2 Corinthians 13:1.

In Ecclesiastes, there is the well-known list of reasons why "two people are better off than one"—if one falls, the other can help him up; if one is cold, the other will warm him; if one is attacked, the other can guard his back. In fact, the writer adds, "three are even better, for a triple-braided cord is not easily broken" (Ecclesiastes 4:9–12). We might think about both of these instructions as being simply practical matters. What we need to realize is that they are practical—that is they work in practical, real life situations—because they are based on a much deeper spiritual reality: the power of one person is intensified and multiplied by the addition of another who is in agreement with that person.

This underlying spiritual reality is revealed in both God's promise of blessing as we obey and curse if we walk away. "Five of you will chase a hundred" (twenty times more than five) "and a hundred of you will chase ten thousand" (a multiplying factor of one hundred!) (Leviticus 16:8). But the multiplier is inherent in life as God created it. Thus, the curse gives the enemy power over God's disobedient people – and the multiplier comes into effect:

> "How could one person chase a thousand of them, and two people put ten thousand to flight, unless their Rock had sold them, unless the Lord had given them up?"
>
> Deuteronomy 32:30

What God is revealing is that—just like the law of gravity which is working whether a person is following the God who designed it or not—there is a law of *multiplication* or *intensification* which is at work whenever two or more people are in agreement. This is true for those agreeing to do good, and for those agreeing to do evil.

But did you also notice what is different about the blessing and the curse? In the blessing, five will chase a hundred (a multiplying or intensification factor of twenty), and a hundred will chase ten thousand (a multiplying factor of *one hundred*!). According to the curse, the multiplier—while still in operation—is only ten. Why? Because "a triple-braided cord is not easily broken". The passage in Ecclesiastes describes the multiplying power of two people who are in agreement, but adds a prophetic riddle. The writer is not describing the addition of a third *person*, but a third *Person*—the Holy Spirit partnering with the two people. And the description reveals *how* the Holy Spirit is present—not beside the two people, but braided together with them. It gives us a picture of what it means to pray *in the spirit*: listening to and responding to the Spirit's direction.

The application is clear: we can grow in our effectiveness in prayer by growing in our ability to listen to the Holy Spirit. And the power of our prayer will be multiplied as we join with others learning how to focus together on one thing at a time, learning together how to listen and respond to the Holy Spirit— the voice behind us.

CHAPTER 7

The Rule of Wrestling

How many years has medical science invested in developing a cure for cancer? How many billions of dollars and millions of man hours? But when it comes to gaining a Kingdom-cure for problems we face, how many of us expect a "one and done" solution?

Think again about an event in Jesus' life we looked at earlier.

When Jesus returned from the mountain where he had been transfigured, clothes and all becoming a "dazzling white," he met the disciples he'd left behind surrounded by a large crowd. The father of a severely demonized boy ran up to Jesus asking him to heal his son because the disciples had been unable to expel the demon. After Jesus had freed the boy from demonic control, the crowd dissipated. Jesus retreated to a house, alone with his disciples. They asked him, "Why couldn't we cast out the evil spirit?" To which Jesus replied, "This kind can be cast out only by prayer" (Mark 9:28–29).

That response is intriguing if you put yourself in the story and think about what happened. When Jesus expelled the demon, *did he pray*? No! He called the evil spirit to pay attention to him, and then he commanded it to come out:

> "Listen, you spirit that makes this boy unable to hear and speak, I command you to come out of this child and never enter him again!"
>
> Mark 9:25

Although Mark doesn't record what the disciples did in their unsuccessful attempts to set the boy free, it's hard to imagine being in their shoes and *not* praying: "O God, help us!"—especially when all their best efforts were having no effect. They were, after all, religious disciples of a God-serving rabbi! Rabbis especially pray and teach their disciples to pray.

But whether or not they prayed, *Jesus did not*. Yet he attributes success in regard to this particular demon to prayer. Why? And what does it mean for your praying?

Consider one other piece of this story: these same disciples had previously been successful in expelling demons. Mark chapter six describes Jesus sending them out and giving them "authority to cast out evil spirits" (Mark 6:7). So, he records, "they went out…and they cast out many demons" (Mark 6:12-18). This is why they were so perplexed at their inability to see the boy set free in this later experience. They were trained, authorized, and had a good record of many successes—possibly unbroken successes.

Jesus pinpoints the cause of their inability: not enough prayer. What his answer reveals is that there are two distinctly different areas of life: prayer (prior to and often out of view) and ministry (sharing the gospel, sharing words of knowledge or wisdom, healing, teaching, leading). Ministry is direct action to bring the will of God into a situation. Prayer is often something we engage in behind-the-scenes, and it affects the results of our subsequent out-in-front ministry actions. Ministry engages *people* on God's behalf: He wants to bring salvation, healing, help, justice into people's lives. Prayer engages *God* on behalf of people.

What Jesus is telling his disciples is that they needed more engagement with God in order to have more of his presence and power in their engagement with people. He's also telling them that the situations they face are not like M&M's—differently colored, but all alike. Some situations yield much more easily than others. Some require a lot more spiritual power than others—and that power is accessed or enlarged as we pray.

I find it equally intriguing that this is apparently *new information* for the disciples. By this point in their training process it would seem like this connection between behind-the-scenes prayer and success in ministry is something Jesus would have covered. Why (apparently) had he not?

I believe this question is reinforced by Luke's report of the timing of Jesus teaching his disciples the famous pattern for prayer we now call "The Lord's Prayer," or "The Our Father." Here is Luke's account: "Once

Jesus was in a certain place praying. As he finished, one of his disciples came to him and said, 'Lord, teach us to pray...'" (Luke 11:1).

In both these stories, Jesus gives them the information about the why and how of prayer because they wanted to know and recognized they *needed* to know. He was ready to teach them what to do when they were ready to do it.

The fact that you are still reading this book on how to pray is evidence of your wanting not simply to learn a few interesting things about prayer, but to pray—with more consistency and greater confidence in its effectiveness.

Prayer is not irrelevant to effectiveness in ministry. Prayer directly affects our ministry effectiveness.

Let's remind ourselves of a revelation about prayer we've already discussed. It is in the letter of James. In chapter 5, he emphasizes the importance of prayer by stating: "The earnest prayer of a righteous person has great power and produces wonderful results" (James 6:16).

There is an equation here. On the one side is behind-the-scenes prayer; on the other side is out-in-front wonderful results. Prayer releases the power of God's kingdom. That power causes real world changes.

One key to increased power and effectiveness in prayer is in the *kind* of prayer: it is not dutiful, beautifully-worded, or repeating the same words over and over prayer; it is *earnest* prayer.

In an earlier chapter, I showed how the way Elijah prayed as recorded in 1 Kings 19, demonstrates what *earnest* looks like; he prayed with his body stooped in the birthing position, and he prayed not once but seven times until he saw the real world indications of the results for which he was praying. The birthing position is a reflection of *intensity*; the number of times reflects *goal-oriented persistence* (that is, Elijah is not praying in order to gain "religious points," but in order to have God grant a particular goal—rain in drought-stricken Israel).

I believe that in order to pray effectively, we must embrace how God reveals effective prayer to us: Effective prayer is wrestling with God.

We began this book with the recognition that as God's temple, we have a God-given name that reveals and decrees our function and destiny: House of Prayer. Do you realize we have another name—a name already given into which we have been grafted? It is the name, Israel.

Here is where it was given:

> "During the night Jacob got up and took his two wives, his two servant wives, and his eleven sons and crossed the Jabbok River with them. After taking them to the other side, he sent over all his possessions. This left Jacob all alone in the camp, and a man came and wrestled with him until the dawn began to break. When the man saw that he would not win the match, he touched Jacob's hip and wrenched it out of its socket. Then the man said, 'Let me go, for the dawn is breaking!'
> But Jacob said, 'I will not let you go unless you bless me.'
> 'What is your name?' the man asked.
> He replied, 'Jacob.'
> 'Your name will no longer be Jacob,' the man told him. 'From now on you will be called Israel, because you have fought with God and with men and have won.'
> 'Please tell me your name,' Jacob said.
> 'Why do you want to know my name?' the man replied. Then he blessed Jacob there.
> Jacob named the place Peniel (which means 'face of God'), for he said, 'I have seen God face to face, yet my life has been spared.' The sun was rising as Jacob left Peniel, and he was limping because of the injury to his hip. (Even today the people of Israel don't eat the tendon near the hip socket because of what happened that night when the man strained the tendon of Jacob's hip.)"
>
> Genesis 32:1–29

Who is this mysterious person who comes to wrestle with Jacob as he is about to enter the land of God's inheritance? While it is possible he was an angel, the more likely assumption is that he is Jesus in his pre-incarnate form. There are at least three reasons for thinking this. First, Jacob says "I have seen God face-to-face." This is particularly significant because on at least two previous occasions he has seen and interacted with angels (Genesis 21:1–2 and Genesis 28:12–17). One of them was just prior to this encounter and took place while he was awake. The first was in a vivid dream in which he saw angels going up and down a stairway that connected earth and heaven. In that dream, he also saw the Lord—distinct from the angels—at the top of the stairway speaking to him. In this wrestling match, Jacob knew this was the Lord because he recognized him from his previous encounters.

A second reason is that the mysterious person will not divulge his name. Throughout the first five books of the Bible, God is laying the foundations upon which the whole of salvation will be built. A significant part of that is God's revelation of his names. Each name reveals an aspect of God's function and destiny—and because it is revealed it forms the basis for faith. For example, we can trust in God's power and promise to heal because he himself revealed that name to his people: "I am the Lord who heals you" (Exodus 15:26).

Salvation takes effect only when two things happen. First when God reveals what he is willing and committed to do; and second when we express what we are willing and committed to receive and in receiving live out. Deuteronomy 29:29 states: "The secret things belong to the Lord our God, but the things revealed belong to us and to our sons forever…"

I am quoting from the New American Standard translation because it succinctly captures the partnership between God and his people. God *reveals* in order that we may know *how to live a life of faith*. Whether a person lived during the period of the Old Testament and its Law, or in the New Testament era and Grace, we live in the unfolding experience of God's salvation by faith. Abraham *believed* what God revealed, and *received* God's gift of a righteous life (Genesis 15:6). That is the beginning of the salvation story. Towards the very end of the Old Testament period, the prophet Habakkuk looks back over the entire story to that point and states: "The righteous will live by his faith" (Habakkuk 2:4). Paul in the New Testament reaffirms this as the absolute heart and foundation of salvation: "This is accomplished from start to finish by faith. As the scriptures say 'The righteous will live by his faith'" (Romans 1:17, NLT, NASB).

What it means to live a life of faith is to discover what God has revealed about Himself, and then to live our lives as if that were in fact true. And this reality is so much larger than we often consider. To grasp this, let me quote the whole of Deuteronomy 29:29—"The secret things belong to the Lord our God, but the things revealed belong to us and to our sons forever, *that we may observe all the words of this law.*"

The great spiritual principle stated here is that what God reveals to us belongs to us (and that is always in the present, because whichever generation first received the revelation, it belongs to every subsequent generation—"our sons forever"). But there is a difference between belonging to us and being experienced by us.

If my father owned a house on a Caribbean island, but kept it a secret, I would never get access to it. But if he had decided that I should inherit it, and at the reading of his will I learned that there was a house, and was given the title documents along with directions about to get there, that house would now belong to me. But I'll never experience it unless I "live by faith." I will have to do something to get to that house, though I've never actually seen it. I will have to spend my money, my energy, and my time differently.

Here is how that analogy demonstrates the spiritual principle.

What God reveals is an aspect of who he is in relation to us. It is an aspect of his unfolding salvation. This is true whether it is "I am the Lord who heals your diseases," or "I am the Lord your God…Thou shalt not commit adultery." Both are a revelation of an aspect of God that we are meant to place our living faith in, and therefore experience as the unfolding of salvation.

God's statement concerning adultery reveals that God does not commit adultery. In the cultures that early Israel lived in the midst of, gods often committed adultery. This prohibition was one of a handful of significant markers by which God was revealing himself as totally distinct from the mythologies and the worship of the surrounding nations. But more than this, God was revealing his own character: he is utterly faithful to his vows of commitment best reflected in the commitment of husband and wife. Rooted in creation ("in his image, male and female…and the two shall become one flesh," Genesis 1:27, 2:24), this theme is repeated over and over throughout the Bible. For example, God describes his relationship to Israel as marriage:

> "And when I passed by again, I saw that you were old
> enough for love. So I wrapped my cloak around you

> to cover your nakedness and declared my marriage vows. I made a covenant with you, says the Sovereign Lord, and you became mine."
>
> Ezekiel 16:8

This same passage describes Israel's disobedience as adultery (Ezekiel 16:17). In a similar accusation, but in a far more dramatic way, God portrays his relationship with Israel by instructing the prophet Hosea to marry a specific woman who is already a prostitute, then to allow her to betray him by returning to prostitution, and finally to buy her back and restore their marriage. Malachi and Ephesians both contain powerful reiterations of God's utter faithfulness to us as revealed in the commitment of marriage. And the closing book of the Bible, the end of the story of our salvation—describes the marriage supper of the Lamb.

The revelation—which now and forever after—belongs to us is "I am the Lord your God…Thou shalt not commit adultery". Now that it belongs to us, in order to experience it (which is an aspect of God's salvation, saving us from darkness, death, and destruction) we must live it out by faith. We must live as though it were true.

On one side of this, it means living in the security of knowing that no matter how much it may seem that God has abandoned us in favor of someone else ("Look at how God is blessing *them*…"), we can trust his commitment forever ("I have loved you with an unfailing love"…"He causes all things to work together for good for those who love him"…"I am convinced that nothing shall separate us from the love of God" (Jeremiah 31:3, Romans 8:28, 38).

On the other side of this, it means living out the revealed character of God in our own lives. Salvation, after all, is *becoming like him*. As Paul describes this, he writes, "Put on your new nature, and be renewed as you *learn to know your Creator* [discovering what he has revealed] and *become like him*" (Colossians 3:10). So, we live in a God-like commitment of faithfulness to our own husband or wife. We do this in faith, trusting that in faithfulness lies the actual experience of salvation, and in adultery—in vow-breaking—lies the inevitable experience of distrust, fearfulness, wounding and woundedness.

We're exploring the edges of a much larger subject, far too extensive to deal with here. The crucial point for developing a deeper understanding of effective prayer is that the Law is not an arbitrary list of do's and don'ts, but a revelation of God the Creator, human beings designed to be like him, and the creation which reflects him. Of course, both humanity and the creation are also broken. It is like looking at a broken bicycle (although immeasurable more complex): we can see how it is *meant* to work, even though it is not working as designed.

What is incredibly significant for understanding the how and why of prayer is that God should engage Jacob in this wrestling match just as Jacob is poised to receive the blessings long promised to him. Jacob has had a handful of encounters where God has spoken and so revealed promises to him: of bringing him back to possess this land promised first to Abraham and his descendants, promises of multiplying his descendants, promises that all the families of the earth will be blessed through them, promises of being master over his brother, promises of protection. These and more are what God has revealed to Jacob, and so they belong to him. But he has not experienced them. In fact, as he draws closer and closer to the place of fulfillment, he is also getting closer and closer to a cutting off of the promise as he approaches Esau, his aggrieved brother whom he knows took a vow to kill him.

What is even more intriguing is that *Jacob prays* just hours before the wrestling match! Some messengers whom Jacob had sent ahead to find Esau and to inform him of Jacob's arrival "hoping you will be friendly," return to tell Jacob that Esau is already on his way "with an army of 400 men."

So Jacob prays:
> "O God of my grandfather Abraham, and God of my father, Isaac—O Lord, you told me 'Return to your own land…' And you promised me, 'I will treat you kindly.' O Lord, please rescue me from the hand of my brother, Esau…"

Genesis 32:9–12

But he does not just "leave it in God's hands." After dividing his whole camp into three groups, he entrusted each of them with substantial gifts to be presented to Esau, hoping to appease him, and sent them ahead. Then he himself stayed behind. Why? Was it in anticipation of an additional time of prayer? Was it because of fear, hoping to preserve his own life even if Esau captured and killed his family and all he owned? The story doesn't tell us. But what the story does tell us is that when Jacob had been left all alone, "a man came and wrestled with him."

The significance of this story is that, to pray effectively, there will be many times when we, too, will need to *wrestle with God*. Prayer is wrestling; wrestling is prayer. A number of details in the story reinforce this in amazing ways.

First, this event is the origin of the name, not just of Jacob, but of the Jewish people: the people of God, the nation in the earth over which he is king, and through whom he is bringing and will bring his kingdom reign.

In the first chapter, we saw that when God names something or someone he is revealing their function and destiny. Jesus, for example, was given by heavenly revelation two names. As God's angel, Gabriel, who "stand[s] in the very presence of God…who send[s] me…" (Luke 1:19), revealed to Joseph, the name of the child conceived in Mary's womb was to be Jesus, meaning "God saves." The name reveals his function and destiny: "he will save his people from their sins" (Matthew 1:21). Jesus' second name, as Matthew tells us immediately following Gabriel's revelation, is Immanuel—the name of the coming Messiah first revealed to and through the prophet Isaiah. That name means "God with us," and likewise reveals another aspect of Jesus' function and destiny to be fulfilled in a way no one could ever anticipate or imagine. In Jesus, God is with us because he became one of us.

In the opening chapter, we saw that God has named us as his temple—the place of his manifest presence on earth. We are called, by God, a "house of prayer," and the name reveals our function and destiny. And here in the very beginnings of our unfolding salvation history, the foundational development of God's salvation—carrying people, God himself comes to wrestle with Jacob and at the climax of the story gives him a new name: Israel. What a revelation!

Jacob means "supplanter" and "deceiver." It is a word in Hebrew that sounds like "heel." The meanings of the name resonate with the character and activity of Satan, whose children in our rebellion we became and whose authority we came under. He is the one who, as revealed to Isaiah and Ezekiel, was created as a magnificently beautiful angel of God and assigned a position of great honor and responsibility as God's agent. But evil entered his heart and, as Isaiah records,

> "You said to yourself, 'I will ascend to heaven and set my throne above God's stars...I will climb to the highest heavens and be like the Most High.'"
>
> Isaiah 14:12–14, cf. Ezekiel 28:11–19

Satan is the one who enticed us to follow and become like him by inviting us to eat from the one tree God had told us to not eat from. But, whispered the serpent, if you eat this fruit, "you will be like God." And so we did, and in doing so became Jacob: a people created in God's image to inherit the earth and bring his blessing throughout all the nations, but who tried to "supplant" God, himself. Rather than being God's agent, we tried to become the Author!

Now, in this story, Jesus—the as-yet unrevealed God-with-us Savior—gives Jacob, and the whole people of God of whom he is the progenitor, a new name: Israel.

What is the meaning of that name? It is a combination of two Hebrew words. The first is a verb meaning "wrestle." The second is "el", the name for God. As the wrestling angel tells Jacob, "From now on your name will be Israel because you have wrestled with God and with men and have won."

Don't miss the two-fold arena of wrestling: it is both in prayer behind-the-scenes (with God) and in ministry where we act to usher in and fulfill what we have prayed for (with men). In fact, it is impossible to pray in faith without being willing to be the answer to your prayers!

In relation to prayer, God has named us Israel. We are not the "Abrahamites," we are the Israelites. *Our function and destiny is to wrestle with God for all he has revealed.* Practically, what does this mean?

Look again at how the story unfolds:

> "This left Jacob all alone in the camp, and a man came and wrestled with him until the dawn began to break. When the man saw that he would not win the match, he touched Jacob's hip and wrenched it out of its socket. Then the man said, 'Let me go, for the dawn is breaking!' But Jacob said, 'I will not let you go unless you bless me.'"

Jacob is holding on to one thing only: he is holding on to God. There is only one thing he will not let go of—God—everything else he has sent ahead. The reality is that the focus of our prayer and what we are wrestling for in every situation is God. What does that mean?

Here is another Biblical example of a great wrestler-in-prayer, Moses, and one of his wrestling matches. It's worth reading from this perspective:

> "One day Moses said to the Lord, 'You have been telling me, Take these people up to the Promised Land. But you haven't told me whom you will send with me. You have told me, I know you by name and I look favorably upon you. If it is true you look favorably upon me, let me know your ways so I may understand you more fully and continue to enjoy your favor. And remember that this nation is your very own people…If you don't personally go with us, don't make us leave this place. How will anyone know that you look favorably on me—on me and on your people—if you don't go with us? For your presence among us sets your people and me apart from all the other people on the earth.'
> The Lord replied to Moses, 'I will indeed do what you have asked.'"
>
> Exodus 33:12–16

Remember where Moses was. He was in the shadow of Mount Sinai, in the middle of a barren wilderness! But he is praying that God not send them to the land flowing with milk and honey, unless his presence goes with them. Moses is saying that being in the desert with God is far better than being in the milk-and-honey land without him.

Every effective pray-er has come to realize that any blessing without his presence is empty. They have come to realize that in prayer we are wrestling not for a blessing of God, but for the God who brings blessing. We need him to come with it. Every request that is *of* God is *for* God.

Think of this in simple, personal terms. Think of a need, an issue, in your own life. You need a house. Are you praying for the house you want, or the house he wants you to have where his presence can reside? Like Moses, we need to pray: "Don't lead me up from here unless you go with me."

Are you praying for the job you want with the higher salary and better benefits, or are you praying for the one God wants where his presence can most powerfully extend his kingdom?

Are you praying for a relationship to develop with that person you are dating, or are you praying that God be the one in whom any relationship be fulfilled?

The heart of the pattern for prayer Jesus gave us is "Your Kingdom come." It is the realization that the answer to every need we pray for is God, himself. And part of wrestling in prayer is pressing God for results, while consciously listening/sensing what the Holy Spirit may be directing—or re-directing—us to pray for.

To wrestle effectively in prayer also means to wrestle *with God* – that is, to wrestle with *who God is*. Let me explain.

Let's return for another look at Abraham's encounter with God in Genesis 18. As we've already shown, this encounter is a God-initiated experience designed to teach all of us how to pray effectively. The situation is this: God, as in the wrestling match with Jacob, comes to Abraham and tells him he is preparing to send judgment on Sodom. Abraham immediately "prays"—that is, he immediately begins talking to God about that decision, asking for a different result. Abraham's interaction with God is a practical example of how to effectively wrestle with God in prayer.

First of all, it says, "Abraham approached him…" (Genesis 18:23). So often we keep ourselves at a safe, discreet distance from God. But God is looking for those who will, as Jesus said, "take the kingdom by force" (Matthew 11:12). He is asking us to "boldly approach the throne of grace" (Hebrews 4:16).

Oswald Chambers helped me grasp what God is looking for from us when he wrote that our imagination is a God-designed part of us, and is a reflection of his own nature. Our imagination is a powerful tool to engage our hearts and focus our minds on an unseen reality. When we pray, therefore, we can use our imagination to stand before the awesome throne of God himself.

How often does Paul tell us in different ways to "set your sights on the realities of heaven, where Christ sits at the place of honor at God's right hand…" (Colossians 3:1)? How many times throughout scripture does God allow someone an experience of heaven's realities, which they then record for us to read and to participate in vicariously—if we will use our imaginations?

> "I saw the Lord. He was sitting on a lofty throne, and the train of his robe filled the Temple…
>
> I watched as thrones were put in place and the Ancient One sat down to judge. His clothing was as white as snow, his hair like purest wool. He sat on a fiery throne with wheels of blazing fire, and a river of fire was pouring out, flowing from his presence. Millions of angels ministered to him; many millions stood to attend him…
>
> I saw a throne in heaven and someone sitting on it. The one sitting on the throne was as brilliant as gemstones—like jasper and carnelian. And the glow of an emerald circled his throne like a rainbow."
>
> Isaiah 6:1; Daniel 7:9–10; Revelation 4:2–3

To approach God in prayer is something we can—and must—do to become increasingly effective in our prayer. Using our imaginations to place ourselves before God's throne is a practical way to focus our minds and hearts on his *nearness*, his awesome, incomparable, immeasurable *majesty* (with whom *nothing* is impossible), and because of and in Jesus his amazing *grace*.

Returning to Abraham's encounter, when he approaches the Lord, he speaks up and says, "Will you sweep away both the righteous and the wicked?…" (Genesis 18:23). With that opening question, Abraham lays out a foundation statement for a lengthy argument. How does this apply to our own praying?

We must not only approach God, but we must then wrestle with him by constructing verbal arguments based on who he is. The basis of Abraham's argument is in verse 25: "Should not the Judge of the whole earth do what is right?" And Abraham doesn't merely state the fact of God's Judge-ship, he constructs his demands using that as a reason God must withhold judgment in this case: "Suppose you find fifty righteous people living there in the city—will you still sweep it away and not spare it for their sakes? Surely you wouldn't do such a thing, destroying the righteous along with the wicked…" I'm not repeating here all the words

Abraham used, nor do I assume all his words are actually recorded in the narrative we now have. What scripture records is typically a condensed, highly focused version of events.

The point is that wrestling in prayer with God is to argue with him for an outcome based on his character and his revealed will and promises. God is looking for active partners, not passive watchers.

While Moses is on Mt. Sinai receiving God's instructions for Israel—the Ten Commandments, the priesthood, the plans for the Tabernacle—the people waiting below make a Golden Calf. God tells Moses what they've done and that he has decided to destroy them and in their place "make you, Moses, into a great nation." Immediately Moses responds, "Change your mind about this terrible disaster you have threatened against your people!" And he constructs a series of arguments which he uses to wrestle with God. His first argument is that the people of Israel are "your own people." His second argument is that God has publically displayed his overwhelming power in Israel's deliverance from Egypt. So "why let the Egyptians say, 'God rescued them with evil intention of slaughtering them...and wiping them from the face of the earth?'" This is an argument based on God's goodness, and his reputation for goodness in the earth.

Moses (the great prayer hero) brings up a *third* argument: God's promises to Abraham, Isaac, and Jacob to make their descendants "as numerous as the stars of heaven," and to give them the land of Israel to "possess...forever." In fact, Moses argues, God not only made these promises, but "you bound yourself with an oath..."

In response to this lengthy argument, based on who God is and what he has already done and specifically promised, God "changed his mind about the terrible disaster he had threatened to bring on his people" (Exodus 32:1-14).

Daniel, another great prayer hero, prays for the restoration of the destroyed Temple and the ruined city of Jerusalem. How? By constructing a long argument based on God's righteous judgments having now been fulfilled, God's promise that the period of judgment would last only seventy years, God's revealed character of mercy, and God's own reputation as a covenant-keeping God (Daniel 9:1–20).

In response, God sends the angel Gabriel to reveal a "Yes, I will… and I'll do even more!" (Daniel 9:21-27).

The early church followed this same pattern when Peter and John were first arrested and told to "never again…speak of…teach in the name of Jesus." On hearing this news, the believers together prayed for a greater release of healing power, signs, and wonders. Their prayer was based on an argument that what the authorities were opposing was God's own plan—therefore God should back up his plan with his power (Acts 4:18-31).

In response, God releases the Holy Spirit. The meeting place is physically shaken and all are filled with the Holy Spirit. They have successfully wrestled with God…and they go out to wrestle with men: "Then they preached the word of God with boldness."

I have cited all these examples because we often dismiss the value of constructing arguments with God in prayer. Yet, the requirement for effective prayer is our personal engagement in the result. The very process of constructing an argument requires us to become more deeply in touch with the situation we're praying for and why God should act as we are asking. In what way does his character and his promises relate to our request? How important is it to us?

Everything I have described in this chapter is intended to help us realize that our natural inclination will be to stop praying about a situation too soon. We need to recognize that we *want* a quick fix, and are quite likely to theologize a reason for that impatience: "God hears every prayer, knows what the real situation is, and will certainly carry out his will in his time. Surely, praying more won't do more. In fact, it may demonstrate a lack of faith…"

What I am arguing is that God's plan for intervention includes and is dependent on people willing to *wrestle* in prayer. My arguments are based on God's biblical revelations. In fact, to what we've already discovered about what wrestling in prayer includes, the Bible adds fasting.

God himself commanded his people to fast at least once each year on the Day of Atonement. Besides that, the Bible is full of references to individual people and whole cities and nations fasting at critical moments. When, for example, a decree had been signed to annihilate the Jewish people throughout the Persian Empire, Esther asks all Jews to fast along with her for three days, after which she will personally appeal to the king for a counter decree. Nehemiah joins fasting with his prayers for God to intervene in the rebuilding of Jerusalem's destroyed walls. Daniel adds fasting to his prayers for an end to Israel's exile in Babylon. The famous worship and prayer meeting at which the Holy Spirit instructed the Antioch church leadership to lay hands on Paul and Barnabas and to send them off on the great missionary venture that evangelized the Roman Empire was worship and prayer accompanied by fasting.

My point is that fasting is not some seldomly-mentioned, reserved-only-for-super-spiritual-giants kind of activity. It is presented in both Old and New Testaments as a normal part of *wrestling in prayer*. Jesus himself taught that fasting was as normal a part of the life of a disciple as is prayer and giving. He put it like this: "When you give, [do it like this, not like that]…When you pray, [do it like this, not like that]…When you fast [do it like this, not like that]…" (Matthew 6:1–18). "*When*"—not "*if*."

Despite what Jesus taught, and despite the witness of the entire Bible, fasting gradually became associated with only especially "spiritual" people (monks, priests, nuns) who viewed the physical body with its appetites and pleasures as evil. Fasting became one way of trying to force the body to "die". While this is an oversimplification, it reflects a common assumption still held by many today. Fortunately, there has been a gradual restoration of the normalcy and necessity of fasting throughout the whole church. As one brief encouragement to this shift in understanding from "super-spiritual" to practical (normal and necessary), look at two passages of scripture.

The first is in Deuteronomy, where Moses reminds the people of Israel what God has done and why:

> "He humbled you by letting you go hungry and then feeding you with manna…He did it to teach you that people do not live by bread alone; rather we live by every word that comes from the mouth of the Lord."
>
> Deuteronomy 8:3

The Hebrew word for "fast' is a word that literally means "to stop [up] the mouth." When you fast, you prevent food (and sometimes water) from entering your mouth. What God is saying in this passage is that he deliberately led them into an enforced fast first of all in order to humble them. There is a connection between our own strength, which is always the source of pride, and food. Food nourishes and maintains our strength. Fasting removes our source of strength. The longer we live without food, the weaker we become. In a very practical way we are *humbled*. We are acknowledging that we are *dependent* creatures.

But God doesn't stop there. He says that the ultimate purpose of this enforced fast was to have them eat manna—a food from the realm of heaven—God's kingdom where his will is always done and always brings life. Manna, God tells them, represents God's heaven-powered words "spoken" into this realm. The renewed strength the people of Israel received as they ate the manna was intended to demonstrate by their own physical experience that "man lives by every word that comes from the mouth of God."

The significance of this is intensified when Jesus, as the new Adam and the new Israel, re-does this very experience immediately following his baptism and being filled with the Holy Spirit. As Luke describes it, Jesus is "driven by the Holy Spirit into the wilderness for forty days." At the end of this "enforced" fast, Jesus is tempted by Satan himself to turn stones into bread—that is, to nourish his own strength. Instead, Jesus responds by quoting the very words recorded in Deuteronomy: "man lives by every word that comes from the mouth of God."

Every time we choose to fast, we are choosing to humble ourselves according to this God-given pattern. We are at the same time saying: "God, it is *your word* from heaven breaking into *our situation* here on earth that is the true and only source of strength." We are casting ourselves upon him in a symbolic and at the same time literal way.

David in Psalm 35 sums up the reason for every Biblical fast: When I prayed for those who were sick, I intensified my prayers by "humbling my soul with fasting" (Psalm 35:13, NASB).

In the Genesis account of Jacob's struggle—this incredible template for wrestling in prayer the requirement of being humbled is clear: "he touched Jacob's hip and wrenched it out of its socket."

Many years ago, a famous pastor, James H. McConkey asked a doctor friend, "What is the exact significance of God's touching Jacob upon the sinew of his thigh?"

The doctor replied, "The sinew of the thigh is the strongest in the human body. A horse couldn't even tear it apart."

"Ah," the pastor said, "I see. The Lord has to break us down at the strongest part of our self-life before he can have his own way of blessing us" (from Ann Voskamp, *One Thousand Gifts*, pg. 138).

Wrestling effectively is a paradox. On the one hand, we must come *boldly* before God's throne. On the other hand, we must come with real humility—You are God. We are not!

> "As the eyes of servants look to hand of their master,
> as the eyes of a maid to the hand of her mistress, so
> our eyes look to the hand of the Lord our God, until
> he is gracious to us."
>
> Psalm 123:2

Sometimes wrestling prayers will be spoken in as normal a way as Abraham arguing with the Lord over Sodom's fate, or as outwardly quiet as Jacob telling the Lord, "I will not let you leave until you bless me." But at other times it will be as loud and emotional as Jesus sometimes was. As Hebrews records it, "While Jesus as here on earth, he offered prayers and pleadings, with a loud cry and tears…" (Hebrews 5:7). If we *always* are loud and emotional when we pray, something is probably unreal and insincere. But if we never express our prayers with loud cries and tears we have probably missed out on what it means to have God's heart of compassion and to know how much we need what only God can give!

There is one final aspect of what it means to wrestle in prayer—or what it means to realize that *to pray is to wrestle*. This part of wrestling is most obvious in Jacob's experience. It is revealed in *how long* Jacob wrestled—all night, "until the dawn began to break"—and *how long Jacob intended to wrestle*—until God agreed to bless him. (As Jacob put it "I will not let you go unless you bless me" (Genesis 32:26).

For me, the most helpful way of understanding the critical importance of persistence in prayer—until God agrees to bless us—is to ask the question, "Why?' Why would persistence in prayer for a long time be so important? Does it fit with God's character and revealed plan of salvation?

Think about this statement from the book of proverbs:

> "An inheritance gained hurriedly at the beginning will
> not be blessed in the end."
>
> Proverbs 20:21, NASB

This is God's law of inheritance. It is as true and inexorable as the law of gravity. Something received too much and too soon will result in ruin later down the line.

Do you realize that we are God's inheritance? Ephesians 1:18 states that "his holy people...are *his* rich and glorious inheritance" (NLT, my emphasis). Over and over again, the Bible reminds us that "we have a priceless inheritance, "as Peter writes, "an inheritance that is kept in heaven for you, pure and undefiled, beyond the reach of change and decay" (1 Peter 1:4). But how often do we realize that God, too, has an inheritance—and that it is *us*?

How long has God wrestled for his inheritance?

As he wrestles for us—so we wrestle for him!

Some years ago, a young father in our church began to get vision for the importance of prayer. Over a period of two or three years as he set aside time in his personal life to pray, at certain times the Lord would break in to make or reinforce a principle of effective prayer.

One of those principles was this issue of persistence.

One day as he was praying, he had a strong mental image of being inside a locker room. But this locker room was different: it was a locker room for angels. And the angels weren't playing some version of football or basketball—they were in a war.

At one end of the locker room was a window opening onto a room where someone was stationed. As my friend watched, he saw this person answer the telephone and receive what my friend knew were orders from headquarters. The person listened, nodded, hung up the phone, and called out the names of two or three angels.

Immediately, those angels strode to the window and were given the orders to go the aid of someone on earth who was in great trouble.

My friend saw many angels receiving orders in this way. He also saw angels returning from these assignments. Many were obviously tired and to some degree battle-scarred. But as they returned, they were weary but proud. After each such engagement, these victorious angels would receive another stripe on the shoulders of their uniform—badges of honor and increasing rank.

But then my friend saw the two or three angels that he'd first seen go off on their mission returning very dejected and clearly wounded. A short while later, new orders came and a few angels were called forward. My friend knew it was for the same person on whose behalf the first angels had been wounded and defeated. My friend saw that the angels who had the first time been eager to take the assignment now were reluctant. Nevertheless, they readied themselves for battle and headed out.

Again, my friend saw them return. This time they were even more dejected and more seriously wounded.

A third time, orders came down regarding this person none of the angels could seem to help. t this time, before the person behind the window could call out the names of these angels, my friend saw everyone in the locker room clear out.

At this point, my friend asked the Lord why the angels assigned to that particular person kept returning defeated. Very clearly, the Lord said, "Because every time the angels get to the battle, the man gives up and stops praying. As long as he prays, they are given strength to defeat the enemy. But when prayer stops, so does their power."

Like many—perhaps most—visions and dreams, God is not showing pictures of real places. He is creating a visual parable to convey a real point. The purpose of my friend's vision was not to show him that there is an angelic locker room somewhere. God's purpose was to convey one very real point: whether we pray or not makes a difference. But more than that, whether we *persist* in praying makes a difference. To begin to pray about something, and then to stop before it is resolved (or before "God agrees to bless" and there is a sense from the Holy Spirit that "it's enough") can abort what God would have done.

George Mueller is one of the greatest heroes of prayer. He wrote down a list of forty people and persistently prayed that each of them would find salvation in Jesus. One by one the people on the list experienced salvation. George Mueller kept praying for those that still resisted. At his death, thirty-eight of the names had been crossed off with a "Thank you, Lord! Hallelujah!" At his funeral, attended by hundreds, those last two individuals gave their lives to Jesus Christ.

To pray is to wrestle. To wrestle is to not let God go until he blesses us!

CHAPTER 8

The Throne and The Lamb

Jamie Wood and her husband Alan are pastors of Family Ministry at a Vineyard church in Birmingham, Alabama. In their book on building a healthy marriage by partnering with the Holy Spirit, *Three Cord Secret*, Jamie includes the following experience. Some years ago she had a Bible study teacher who told her that whenever she heard the siren of an emergency vehicle, she would immediately pray for those involved. That struck Jamie as very proactive, and from that point on when she heard one, no matter whom she was with, she would take a moment to pray. Since her children were often in the car with her, they would do this together. She writes:

"Once our family was on a trip to Destin, Florida, and we were going out to dinner. A terrible accident had just occurred in front of a bank. There was a car that was so flattened in the front that it looked impossible to have any survivors, but we prayed for any occupants of the car. For months, the Lord brought pictures of that accident to mind along with the thoughts of the driver. I would pray, but I remember thinking, *I don't even think that this person could have survived.* Still, I would pray. About six months later, I was talking to a woman at my church, and she told me of this school teacher friend from the Homewood School system who was in this horrific accident in Destin, Florida. She told of how her friend had gone to an

ATM machine for some cash at dinnertime, and how this accident had almost taken her life.

After a long recovery, she went back to her elementary teaching job where she would impact many young lives. As the date, time, and location had been confirmed, I *knew* it was the accident we had seen. God is faithful to reward *our* faithfulness. When I think back on how this even came up in our conversation, I can't recall. All I know is that God made a way for us to find out because He wanted us to know that our prayers were heard and honored. To this day, I tell my children when we hear a siren, you never know, you may be praying for the life of your future spouse."

Did Jamie's prayer really affect the outcome, or was all of it—the timing of her presence near the accident scene, the woman's recovery, the connection with the friend who later told Jamie—simply coincidence?

Someone once said, "People tell me that so-called answers to prayer are just coincidence. Perhaps that's so. But I have discovered that the more I pray, the more coincidences seem to happen."

The Bible never attaches prayer to *coincidences*; it always attaches them to *consequences*. It never instructs us to pray less; it universally challenges us to pray more. "*Prayer*," writes Dallas Willard, "is God's arrangement for a safe *power sharing* with us in his intention to bless the world through us" (*Knowing Christ Today*, p. 160).

Prayer is power sharing because, as a consequence of our prayer God will release his power. Without that prayer, his power is not released. And it is *safe* power sharing because any release of God's power will only happen according to his will. Therefore, as Dallas Willard continues, "in response to prayer we see good accomplished far beyond what we are capable of [God's power shared with us] and in a form suited to the wisdom of God—not just to what we think *we* know about the situation we are praying for [*safe* because only in accord with his will]. Clearly, prayer is a major dimension of living interactively with God."

The reason we can attribute answers to prayer as mere coincidence is that we can only see prayer from earthside. In the Bible, God has given us some heavenside views of prayer. The exercise and development of faith has to do with taking these heavenside views seriously and acting as though they are true (which they are!). One of those heavenside views that has been of enormous help to me is what I call "The Throne and The Lamb." I share it in the hope that it will be of similar help to you.

This heavenside view begins with the familiar verse from Hebrews:
> "So, let us come boldly to the throne of our glorious God. There we will receive his mercy and we'll find grace to help us when we need it most."
>
> Hebrews 4:16

What we often fail to realize about this highly visual encouragement to pray for a release of God's power (power sharing) whenever we are confronted with a need, is that all prayer is in fact *coming before God's heaven-located* throne.

The issue is not whether whenever we pray we are coming before God's throne. The issue is: will we come *boldly*!

The history of the church is filled with a singular lack of understanding about this. Those of us who are "normal" people try to get someone "better positioned" to present our requests before God's throne. We can perhaps get the attention of a "saint" or of Mary, or of a pastor or priest. The reality is this: whenever any one of us prays we are standing before God's throne.

When the apostle John is taken in the spirit into heaven, he sees God seated on a great throne. Among those who are present with him are twenty-four elders. Each of them has a golden bowl "filled with incense, *which are the prayers of God's people*" (Revelation 5:8). Two pieces of this description are significant. The first is that the prayers are not "of the holiest of saints" or some other group of highly regarded "spiritual" people. No. These prayers are those prayed by any and every person who is a member of "God's people."

The second significant piece of this description is that all these prayers are right before God's throne. The picture John sees is intended to reveal this about prayer when viewed from heavenside: every person's prayer is before the throne of God. How many of all the prayers prayed actually come before the throne? As John describes it, not "some of the payers," but rather "*the* prayers." They are not measured, evaluated, sorted and culled. They are *prayed*, and as prayed they are present before the awesome throne of God.

God is revealing this because he wants us to value every one of our prayers with the value he places on them. Imagine if each time you wanted the power of the U.S. government to be deployed, you only needed to say "Mr. President," and instantly you would find yourself in the Oval Office standing before the President's desk. As you appear, he looks up at you and says "Yes? What is on your mind?" "Well, sir, there's a situation that I believe needs your attention…"

That is exactly what the Bible is revealing happens when each of us prays. "Our Father…" we begin, and instantly we are standing before the Sovereign over all creation and every nation. The only difference is that we can't see with our earthside eyes our new location. God reveals it to us so that we can pray in the absolute confidence that we are standing right in front of his throne.

Why his *throne*? What is so significant about being before his throne as we pray?

A throne represents the authority of a ruler to rule. And more than that, it is the place where ruling decisions are made.

To come before his throne is to present a situation "needing your attention." It is asking for a decision to be rendered and then a decree to be made and carried out. It is to come to the place which has jurisdiction over everything and everyone. And when a ruler seats himself on his throne he is saying I am now ready to hear requests and render decisions.

The very first time the throne of God is mentioned in the Bible is in the book of Exodus. Israel has been delivered from Egypt and is traveling towards Mt. Sinai, when suddenly they are attacked by warriors from nearby Amalek. After Joshua and his troops defeat them, the Lord himself tells Moses to write these words on a scroll and read them aloud to Joshua: "I will erase the memory of Amalek from under heaven." Then Moses explains "They have raised their fist against God's throne, therefore the Lord will be at war with them generation after generation" (Exodus 17:14, 16).

One meaning of the word throne is the heaven-located seat of God's authority to make and then carry out decrees on earth. In his authority—his throne—God has decreed that Israel shall be his people. He is carrying that out by delivering them from Egypt and Pharaoh's power, and is now leading them by cloud and fire to the place he wants them to inhabit by a route he himself has determined. To attack Israel is to fight against God's throne—his authority to make decrees, and the decrees he has made and is carrying out.

This is precisely the reason the pharisee, Gamaliel gives the advice he does when counseling the Jewish religious leaders not to execute Peter and John in the very early days of the church's expansion in Jerusalem: "My advice is, leave these men alone. Let them go. If they are planning and doing these things on their own, it will soon be overthrown. But if it is from God, you will not be able to overthrow them. You may even find yourself fighting against God" (Acts 5:38–39).

By fighting against the people of God, says Moses (and Gamaliel repeats), "they have raised their fist against God's throne." This reveals the intimate and continuous connection between heaven and earth: it is *us* as God's people. And grasping this impacts our confident boldness as we pray.

If we feel—and believe we are—distant and disconnected from God and his throne, we will pray rarely and with little confidence.

Knowing this, Paul tells us to see ourselves *where* we really are:
"Since you have been raised to a new life with Christ, *set your sights on the realities of heaven*, where Christ sits at the place of honor at God's right hand [seated on his throne]…your real life is hidden with Christ in God (Colossians 3:1, 3). You must love as *citizens of heaven* (Philippians 1:27). For he raised us from the dead along with Christ and seated us with him in the heavenly realms because we are united with Christ Jesus."

Ephesians 2:6

All this impacts far more than just how we pray! It impacts everything about all our life. But the impact *includes* how we pray! It is something God himself wants us to "see" every time we pray, because every time we pray we are standing before his throne. God has determined to share his power with us.

But what about *safe* power sharing? Have you prayed something with great fervor and later thanked God that he *didn't* answer that prayer?

I still remember having my third grade Sunday School teacher tell our class "to be very careful what you pray for!" She was a kindly, older woman, perhaps somewhat overweight. And that morning she told us how she had recently prayed earnestly for some strawberry ice cream. She later opened her freezer to discover (as I remember it) one whole quart of strawberry ice cream. She knew it hadn't been there before she prayed—but there it was. And because it was right in her freezer as an answer to her prayer, she ate, not one small bowl, but the entire container. Thus, the lesson: be careful what you pray for.

Even then I was somewhat suspicious of the idea that God would give us whatever we (earnestly "in faith") prayed for. It seemed too dangerous.

This unsafe power sharing was countered by an opposite teaching that we could only pray with the stipulation "if it be thy will." And what God's will might be in very many situations was quite inscrutable.

The result was a decided lack of boldness and authority in prayer. On the one hand, there were many strawberry ice cream prayers that probably ought not be answered; and on the other there was the matter of God's will—since we rarely if ever could be certain what it was, prayer seemed much more religious devotion than results-targeted power sharing.

Gaining boldness begins with the recognition that whenever I pray I am standing before God's throne. He is listening because he wants to share his power with me to effect a different outcome on earth than there would otherwise be. He is helping me become more and more a partner fully in line with his will. Prayer is a journey not only of seeing changed results out there, but of seeing changed results *in here*—in the ways I think, perceive understand, and act. It is a journey of becoming more and more like Jesus—the one who only did what he saw the Father doing (John 5:19), the one who only asked according to and always carried out the Father's will (Hebrews 10:5–7).

The prayer of authority comes from our place in Jesus.

When Jesus tells his disciples that those who follow him will do the things he did, and even greater things, he is specifically including the power sharing results of prayer:

> "I tell you the truth, anyone who believes in me will
> do the same works I have done, and even greater

works, because I am going to be with the Father. You can ask for anything in my name, and I will do it, so that the Son can bring glory to the Father. Yes, ask me for anything in my name, and I will do it!"

John 14:12-14

Jesus is deliberately handing over to his disciples—then and now—a working key to increased authority and effectiveness in prayer: *in my name*. What does that mean practically? Here are three aspects of praying in his name that we need to grasp and implement:

First, "in my name" means "things that glorify me," because then "the Son can bring glory to the Father." Earlier in his ministry Jesus described God's strategy in sending him: the Father is giving his authority to Jesus "so that everyone will honor the Son, just as they honor the Father" (John 5:23). By living lives and praying prayers that are continually aimed at bringing glory to the name of Jesus Christ, we will be continually increasing in our boldness and authority in every prayer. Keep your eyes on this one thing: it is the name of *Jesus* before whom every knee will bow and every tongue will confess out loud—He is the Lord (Philippians 2:9-11). Our task is to pray for things that will increase and extend the honor of his name. The power sharing of God will always have this purpose.

Second, to pray "in my name" means to pray according to the revealed meaning of his name. As we saw in Chapter 8, when Jacob wrestled with "a man" and asked his name, the man refused to give it. A significant reason for believing the man was in fact Jesus in his pre-incarnate form is that revealing that name would be the release of the function of the name's meaning. Until his birth in our flesh-and-blood form, God was not ready to release that function. As the writer of Hebrews explains:

> "Because God's children are human beings—made of flesh and blood—the Son also became flesh and blood. For only as a human being could he die, and only by dying could he break the power of the devil, who had the power of death. Only in this way could he set free all who have lived their lives in slavery to the fear of dying."

Hebrews 2:14–15

When the angel Gabriel tells Joseph that his virgin wife-to-be is carrying a child conceived in her womb by the Holy Spirit, he tells him to give the child the name, Jesus, because the meaning of the name is God saves. The child will carry that name because he will save God's people from their sins—from the power of sin to control them and from the effects of their sins to lead them into death. Therefore, to pray in Jesus' name is to pray for God's saving power to be released in the lives of people still in captivity. We have the authority to pray for God's salvation from sin's power and sin's effects everywhere and always because this is the once-hidden, but now revealed, purpose of God for the earth in the coming of Jesus. His function and his destiny is to be its Savior.

It is also significant to recognize that when Gabriel came to Joseph to reveal Jesus' name as "God saves", Matthew added:

> "All of this occurred to fulfill the Lord's message through his prophet: 'Look! The virgin will conceive a child! She will give birth to a son, and they will call him Immanuel, which means, 'God is with us.'"
>
> Matthew 2:22–23

How does this practically apply to learning to pray with authority? One consequence is this: any prayer for an increase in God's presence will always be in accord with his will. Here are a few implications.

Throughout Jesus' thirty-three years of life in Israel, he was "God with us." Just days before his death on the cross, Jesus himself said, "If you have seen me, you have seen the Father" (John 14:9). But in preparing his disciples for the end of his time with them, he said, "but in fact, it is best for you that I go away, because if I don't The Advocate [the Holy Spirit] won't come. If I do go away, I will send him to you…You know him because he lives with you now and later will be in you" (John 16:7; 14:17b). In the same way (though not the same form) that God was with us in Jesus on earth, so God is now with us in the Holy Spirit on earth. In fact, this part of God's unfolding plan to bring his kingdom is "better" than having Jesus now with us as he was two thousand years ago: then God was with us by being around us; now he is with us by actually being in us!

What may we therefore pray for with authority? We can pray for all who put their faith in Jesus to be filled (and filled and filled and filled) with the Holy Spirit. We can pray for the Holy Spirit to carry out every one of his revealed functions—for example "convicting the world of sin, righteousness, and judgment" (John 16:8), "guiding us into all truth" (John 16:13), revealing things that Jesus wants us to know (John 16:14), distributing spiritual gifts so that our gathered meetings are filled with the supernatural (prophecy, healing, spirit-inspired teaching, etc.) (1 Corinthians 12-14).

And we can always with authority invite the Holy Spirit to come and be present in full and tangible ways. We can pray, "Come, Holy Spirit" and be absolutely certain we are praying in accord with God's will. It is his revealed will to be God-with-us.

There is a third aspect of praying in Jesus' name that can have a major impact on the increase of our personal authority as we pray. It is revealed in the wonderful vision John was given as recorded in the book of Revelation involving the throne of God:

> "Then I saw a scroll in the right hand of the one who was sitting on the throne. There was writing on the inside and the outside of the scroll, and it was sealed with seven seals. And I saw a strong angel, who shouted with a loud voice: 'Who is *worthy* to break the seals on the scroll and open it?' But no one in heaven or on earth or under the earth *was able* to open the scroll and read it.
> Then I began to weep bitterly because no one was found *worthy* to open the scroll and read it. But one of the twenty-four elders said to me, 'Stop weeping! Look, the Lion of the tribe of Judah, the heir to David's throne, has won the victory. He is worthy to open the scroll and its seven seals.'
> Then I saw a Lamb that looked as if it had been slaughtered, but was now standing between the throne and the four living beings…"
>
> Revelation 5:1–6

A simple way to understand the meaning of the scroll is as the Title Deed to the creation begun in Genesis 1:1. Although with Adam's rebellion the creation was corrupted and "subjected to futility" (Romans 8:20), there is written in the scroll God's original function and destiny.

Only man could subject the creation to futility; only man can redeem it into full obedience to the Father's will and to his carefully determined destiny. But as John looks at the sealed scroll, he realizes that no one among all humanity has ever been found who can rightfully take superceding authority over and thus rule over the fulfillment of that destiny.

At that bleakest of moments, he hears the declaration: "Wait! Stop weeping! There is one who has been found worthy. He has won the victory. Look, it is the Lion of the tribe of Judah." John doesn't record what he thought at that moment, but the way it is written suggests that he might have thought: "At last, a superior *power*. The kind of regal power resident in the Lion."

The surprise is that what he sees is not a Lion, but a Lamb—and a Lamb looking as though it has been slaughtered. Instead of superior power, the Lamb has conquered by the sacrifice of his own life for that of the undeserving. As Paul writes, the victory has been won by the foolishness of the cross: not my life of perfect obedience and my rights before God's throne, but my life and my rights given up so they can be transferred to those bound to death whose rights have been forfeited. The scroll and creation's destiny have not been taken back by superior power, instead they have been bought back at the full price of the Lamb's life and his rights.

> "You are worthy to take the scroll and break its seals and open it. For you were slaughtered, and your blood has ransomed people for God from every tribe and language and people and nation. And you have caused them to become a Kingdom or priests for our God. And they will reign on the earth."
>
> Revelation 5:9–10

Our authority in prayer is in the name of Jesus—that is, in the heart of the Lamb who was slain, because it is as the Lamb that Jesus won and is carrying out his victory. We always have the Lamb's authority to pray his heart of mercy over judgment. In truth, this is the age of God's mercy unveiled—even to the unfathomable measure of the gift-sacrifice of God's own and only Son.

Think of it: in the very experience of being crucified, Jesus prays. Boldly he comes before the throne and asks for his Father's decision and decree—not "Set me free at the expense of these my enemies," but "Set my enemies free: Father, forgive them." It is the heart of the Lamb.

Stephen prayed according to that heart for those stoning him: "Lord, don't charge them with this sin." It is the heart of the Lamb who was slain.

Paul, one of those for whom Stephen prayed, having received the Lamb's undeserved forgiveness, describes how he now prays for those who have persecuted him and had him imprisoned, who have had him thrown out of synagogues and cities, who have caused him to be beaten:

> "Dear brothers and sisters, the longing of my heart and my prayer to God is for the people of Israel to be saved."
>
> Romans 10:1

It is the heart of the Lamb who was slain to release the grace of God for all those who have forfeited it.

Isn't this where all the lessons of our authority in prayer began? Where God shared with Abraham his imminent judgment of Sodom as an invitation to take that knowledge and come before him in prayer asking for God's mercy over judgment on his enemies.

We never need to wonder when praying for a rebellious child or an unrighteous king whether God desires to release mercy or judgment. He may be required to at last bring judgment; but his heart is revealed in the heart of the Lamb: it is mercy he longs to give. Our great privilege is to bring the undeserving before his throne for always grace. It is the *throne of grace*. We have been given eternal access to that throne by the grace of the Lamb. We have his authority to ask for that same grace to be extended, expanded, and magnified to all people "from every tribe and language and people and nation." It is a prayer God wants to answer.

This great power sharing plan of God places the great responsibility on us to pray for his grace to be released where it now is absent and is so needed. He is seated on the throne in anticipation of our appearance.

CHAPTER 9

Authority to Pray for Nations

An attitude I have encountered over and over again is this: "I don't want to bother God with my little requests." The other side of this coin is, "I'm too insignificant to pray for really big things—like the issues facing America, or like opening the nation of Spain to the Gospel."

Jesus confronts this attitude on many occasions. For example, in Matthew chapters 6 and 7, Jesus shares a whole series of things about prayer:

First, he says, "When you pray...pray to your Father in private. Then your Father, *who sees everything*, will reward you" (Matthew 6:6).

What Jesus is telling us is that God sees and is very interested in every person who prays. Any time anyone prays, our Father is intimately aware of it, sees that person, and hears that person's prayers. In fact, he is *so* interested in what that person prays, that he will *reward* that individual for taking the time to pray.

Later, Jesus re-emphasizes our importance to God and the importance of our personal needs by telling us "not to worry about everyday life—whether you have enough food and drink, or enough clothes to wear." And why shouldn't we worry? Because "look at the birds. They don't plant or harvest or store food in barns, for your heavenly Father feeds them. And aren't you far more valuable to him than they are?" (Matthew 6:25–26).

Jesus is directly attacking the common feeling we have that who we are and what we need is insignificant in relation to God. And then Jesus says this: "Keep on asking, and you will receive what you ask for. Keep on seeking…keep on knocking…[Because] your heavenly Father [will] give good gifts to those who ask him" (Matthew 7:7, 11:6).

The Father *knows*; the Father *cares*; the Father *gives* to those who ask.

What are the things God encourages us to pray for? Or, to put it another way, what things has God given us *the authority* to pray for?

From the statements of Jesus already quoted, it certainly includes our personal, practical needs. But think for a minute about the pattern for praying that Jesus gave his disciples and which is also a part of Jesus' teaching here in Matthew:

"Pray like this:" Jesus says, "Our Father who is in heaven, hallowed be your name. Your Kingdom come. Your will be done on earth as it is in heaven. Give us this day our daily bread…" (Matthew 6:9–11, NASB).

What is included in the things we have authority to ask God for? Daily bread sorts of things. Simple, personal, practical requests. And also Kingdom-of-God-taking-effect-here-on-earth sorts of things. And there is no apparent limit to what this might include. In fact, Jesus is deliberately raising our sights to include asking for all of God's ruling power in heaven to be released in any and every place on earth.

By juxtaposing God's kingdom, heaven, earth, and our daily bread, Jesus is revealing how integrated and important everything is—from the very large to the very small. According to Jesus the only question is will we use it or will we forfeit it? We have authority to pray for it all.

This is the repeated revelation about prayer throughout the Bible.

In the letter written by Jesus' brother, James, who presided over the first church in Jerusalem, he states:

"Are any of you suffering hardships? *Pray*!
Are any of you happy? Sing praises! (*pray-ses*)
Are any of you sick? Call for the elders to come and *pray* for you.
Such a prayer offered in faith will heal the sick and the Lord will make you well."

James 5:13–15a

Pause for a moment and reflect on what James is saying: If you are in trouble, pray about the troubles. Ask for God's intervention for you personally.

If you are experiencing blessing, pray about that too. Voice your personal praises to God, because, as James has noted earlier in the letter, "Whatever is good and perfect comes down to us from God our Father" (James 1:16). The specific details of our lives are as important to God as they are to us. We have the authority to pray about all of them. And we have the authority (and the need) to ask others—even leaders in the church—to pray for us when we are sick.

Do you see how utterly opposite this is to the attitude that says, "I don't want to bother God (or his leaders who have more important things to do) with my little requests"?

But James doesn't stop with that. After encouraging us to deal with any sin issues through confessing to one another and then praying for one another, forgiving and receiving forgiveness, James writes, "The earnest prayer of a righteous person has great power and produces wonderful results. Elijah was as human as we are [or as the NASB has it, 'a man with a nature like ours], and yet when he prayed earnestly that no rain would fall, none fell for three and a half years! Then, when he prayed again, the sky sent down rain and the earth began to yield its crops" (James 5:16b–18).

Prayer for needs and prayer for nations are spoken in the same breath. There simply is no distinction in the authority given.

Why did James use Elijah as an example for normal followers of Jesus when describing when we should pray and what sorts of things we should pray for?

First, because he could be sure his readers knew he wasn't making this up. This was a real person and a real event. It was part of their well-known history. It actually happened. God is interested in things actually happening—not in some "spiritual exercise." A second reason is everyone knew that, in praying, Elijah was carrying out God's will. What God wanted was a drought, then a pubic prayer contest between those who prayed to Baal and Elijah who prayed to God. When prayers to Baal resulted in nothing while Elijah's prayer was answered, then God wanted the drought broken and rain to return to Israel. The story establishes the purpose of prayer: to have God's will done on the earth.

The downside of Elijah as an example, as James well knew, is that his readers (including us today) might say, "Yes…but I'm no Elijah!" Therefore, James quickly adds that Elijah was "a man with a nature like ours." The sole requirement for praying is being human. Elijah became an effective pray-er seeing wonderful results by *doing it*—by praying. Anyone born can pray, but effective pray-ers are made not born.

Leonard Ravenhill once told the story of a group of tourists visiting a picturesque village in Great Britain. They walked by an old man sitting beside a fence. One of the tourists asked him, "Were any great men born in this village?" The old man looked up at them and replied, "Nope, only babies." Effective pray-ers are made not born—but all of us are born with the capacity to pray.

A Hollywood talent scout once reported this after seeing Fred Astaire: "Can't act. Can't sing. Can dance a little." We are all of a like nature. To begin with all of us can pray a little. God's encouragement is to just do that and see what you'll become. Our authority to pray, like Elijah's, includes personal needs *and* nations.

God's revelation of our authority to pray for nations starts with the very beginning of salvation history when God chooses one man out of the nations to become God's missionary nation—a nation which God will establish and bless so that through them he can bless every nation—"all the families of the earth" (Genesis 12:3).

In other words, one man, Abraham, is the beginning of God's salvation coming to all the nations of the world. And in the subsequent interactions between Abraham and God there is a revelation of what this means as descendants of Abraham—whether by genealogy or by faith. As Paul explains, "Abraham was, humanly speaking, the founder of our Jewish nation…" That is, every Jewish person is a descendant of Abraham by genealogy. But in addition, "Abraham is the spiritual father of those who have faith…the same kind of faith Abraham had…Abraham is the father of all who believe" (Romans 4:1, 11b, 16b).

Here is the crucial application to you and me: God gave Abraham a promise (I will bless all the families of the earth through you and your descendants), and with that promise responsibility (to have faith in God—a faith that listens for God's direction and responds in obedience), and with that responsibility authority. What kind of authority? The authority to pray for nations. Because it is the authority to pray for the promise!

Let me explain this in a bit more detail so that we can understand with a bit more depth of conviction and act in greater confidence.

In Abraham God set in motion his plan to restore all the earth to his rulership. In expressing the first outlines of that plan, God reveals that this restoration will include "all the families of the earth." That is, his plan is not to eradicate all, most, or even some of the nations, but to bless all with his salvation. This great promise made to Abraham in Genesis 12, Paul summarizes in these words: "God's promise [was] to give the whole earth to Abraham and his descendants" (Romans 4:13a).

It is absolutely vital to grasp both that as Abraham's descendants we are being given the whole earth, and that all the nations of the earth are not being destroyed so that we can take over, but that all the nations are being saved. In the words of John's Apocalypse, the kingdoms of the world are not being systematically exterminated, instead they are becoming "the kingdom of our Lord and of his Christ" (Revelation 11:15b). This fulfills all the promises woven throughout the story which begins with Abraham. "Then the sovereignty, power, and greatness of all the kingdoms under heaven will be given to the holy people of the Most High. His kingdom will last forever, and all rulers will obey him" (Daniel 7:27). "I will give you the nations as your inheritance, the whole earth as your possession..." (Psalm 2:8). "To all who are victorious, who obey me to the very end, to them I will give authority over all the nations. They will rule the nations..." (Revelation 2:27). When history has been brought to its climax at the return of Jesus Christ, he will establish his dwelling in the new Jerusalem which will be full of God's visible glory. "The nations [have not been wiped out, but] will walk in its light, and the kings of the world will enter the city *in all their glory*... And all nations will bring *their glory and honor* into the city" (Revelation 21:22–26 selected, my emphasis). There are numerous references similar to these throughout the Bible. And, yes, there are also numerous descriptions of judgment and destruction for nations who embrace evil and reject God's invitation. The crucial point, however, is that God's promise is *blessing for all nations*. And this has significant implications for our *responsibility* and our *authority*.

Let me make this crucial point in one other way. God's call (and promise) to Abraham was that he would *bless* the nations, not that he would *replace* the nations. As the promise-bearer, Abraham was given the responsibility to engage in the fulfillment of that promise.

Remember, God's strategy is always promise, responsibility and authority, because we are partners with him. And in each of those places we can become partners, or can forfeit our partnership!

Abraham is our model. Was it enough for God to give Abraham the promise and for Abraham to hear it? Of course not. Abraham had to believe it. And to believe the promise was far more than giving mental assent. To believe was to act in accordance with the promise and the Promiser.

In Genesis chapter 15 there is recorded a statement which becomes the *sine qua non* of life lived with God, of the eternal life which much later Jesus makes available, calling it the "born-from-above" life (John 3:3, 7–8). "*Sine qua non*" is a Latin phrase meaning "without which not." It is the indispensable condition or element of something, *without which it cannot be*.

Here is the *sine qua non* of receiving God's promise/salvation: "And Abram believed the Lord, and the Lord counted him as righteous because of his faith" (Genesis 15:6).

But this kind of belief or faith in the promise and the Promiser carries with it the responsibility to act on the promise and with the Promiser.

In the Biblical account of Abraham there are seven major points at which faith requires response—the responsibility to act according to faith. They are an outline of the response-ability each of us will need to respond to and act on to carry out and partner in the fulfillment of God's promises. Briefly, here they are:

(1) Genesis 12:4
What will you do with your land and family?
God's first test of faith for Abraham was this: "In order to receive my promise, you must leave *your* land and *your* family." As Jesus restates this, "If you love your father or mother more than you love me, you are not worthy of being mine..." (Matthew 10:37).

(2) Genesis 3:8–11
What will you do with your position of honor?
This test occurs when conflict arises between Abraham's servants and those of his nephew, Lot,

over pastures and water for their cattle and sheep. Will Abraham assert his "rights" as God's promise-bearer, or will he humble himself and defer to his nephew? As Jesus reframes this, he washes the feet of his disciples then says, "Since I, your Lord and Teacher, have washed your feet, you ought to wash each other's feet. I have given you an example to follow" (John 13:14–15).

(3) Genesis 14:18–20
What will you do with your financial income?
After serving Lot again by rescuing him, his family and his flocks from a foreign military raid, Abraham is met by a "priest of God" named Melchizedek. As explicitly described by the New Testament writer of Hebrews, this person represents Jesus Christ himself. To him, and through him to God his Promiser, Abraham immediately gives a tithe of all he has gained by his victory.

How we view our financial income reflects and tests how we understand our partnership with God and his promises. Do we act as though our income is a result of our hard work so we get to decide how much of it we give? Or, like Abraham, do we recognize we fought the battle to receive the income (our hard work), but God is the one who has partnered with us by giving us our talents, our energy, and the favor to obtain results? Giving a tithe—which means "a tenth"—is God's way of letting us recognize we are partners with him in the promises given. It is the amount from our income which God says "belongs to me" (Malachi 3:8–12).

(4) Genesis 16:2–6
What will you do with unfulfilled promises?
The indispensible condition of receiving God's promises I've already said is Genesis 15:6, "And Abram *believed* the Lord, and the Lord counted

him as righteous *because of his faith.*" But this event in Abraham's life did not occur until a number of years after receiving God's promise and passing the first test—taking the responsibility to leave land and family. The details of the story don't tell us how many years had gone by, but we know it had been long enough for Abraham to tell God how frustrated he feels at the lack of fulfillment, and how impossible it is beginning to seem that the promise might be fulfilled. Over and over again, the Bible highlights this important test in the lives of God's promise-partners. In the Psalms there is a very helpful comment about the purpose of promise and delay: "Until the time came to fulfill his dreams [the dreams give to him by God as promises], the Lord tested Joseph's character" Psalm 105:19. A contemporary English version that tries to more directly translate the original Hebrew text is this: "Until the time that his word came to pass, the word of the Lord tested him" (NASB). God's promises if delayed long enough become a test of our character. They force us to keep on choosing to believe in God, or to stop believing. In fact, the test is not simply *revealing* what our character is, but *shaping* what our character is meant to become: the character of a true partner with God who trusts in him and will continue to choose to trust him no matter what the circumstance.

(5) Genesis 17:10–11

What will you do with non-rational commands? God once again reiterates his promise to Abraham, then he tells him to act in responsibility by being circumcised and to circumcise every male in his household…in every generation. With the advantage of hindsight, God's command makes a lot of sense. The promise is descendants; the required response is to act out a covenant sealed with blood with the physical member through which the promise must be fulfilled. In addition, it symbolizes the removal of our human nature descended from Adam which through disobedience became dead to God's way of life. It symbolizes first a "circumcision of the heart" (Romans 2:29 NASB), and then the ultimate circumcision performed by Christ on the cross—"the cutting away of [our] sinful nature" (Colossians 2:11b).

But when God called Abraham to do this, Abraham didn't know, nor could he know, all it would mean. The test was—and for us will be—to act on something which will only make sense in the future.

(7) (Yes, I'm skipping #6. I will come back to it because the sixth test is the heart of the authority to pray this chapter is focusing on.)

Genesis 22:1–19

What will you do with your ministry?

This is the only one of the seven that the Bible specifically identifies with the word "test": "Sometime later, God tested Abraham's faith…" (Genesis 22:1). It is easy to recognize—again, with hindsight—the incredible significance in God's command to Abraham to sacrifice Isaac. The very words underline it: Abraham's name means "father of many." It was a name deliberately given to him by God himself after the fifth test. It is a name which clearly is meant to reaffirm the call of Adam, God's original partner as God's image and likeness, to "be fruitful and multiply" (Genesis 1:27–28). As God intervenes in order to bring about a restoration of humanity, he reveals this will be far more than simply a return to what once was. It will be something greater and better than. In the place of Adam's responsibility (partnering to fulfill God's promise) to "be fruitful," the promise to Abram is, I am changing your name to Abraham because "I will make you *extremely* fruitful" (Genesis 17:5b).

Abraham's name is intended to secure his significance as image and representative of God the Father. Therefore, in the call to sacrifice his son, Abraham is prefiguring the reality that to fulfill the promises of God will require God the Father to sacrifice his Son. And to underline this reality, God calls Abraham to do this with these words: "Take your son, your only son…whom you love so much" (Genesis 22:2a).

That this was the last and greatest test for Abraham is clear. But in what way, as Abraham's descendants, can this be a representative of a test for us?

In 1975 as the founder and president of a media and electronics company, I was faced with a growing sense of a life-changing decision I needed to make. For years my life had revolved around film-making, music, stories and multi-media—all aimed at fulfilling what I believed was God's call to me: to display the reality of Jesus and the Gospel in creative new ways. We had seen some success and were excited about two major projects we were working on. But the needed resources to complete them were always tantalizingly beyond our reach. In fact, it seemed as though they were being closed off instead of opened up. One of the projects had gone through a protracted negotiation with the major Christian music company Word Records. During the process of our negotiations, Word was sold to ABC. At the time, that seemed positive because it increased the financial resources available. On the Friday we were scheduled to sign the final contract to begin production, I received a call from Word's leading producer. He said "I am leaving Word to start my own company, and I'm taking with me all the artists you are using in your production. That means Word is no longer interested.

As a start-up company, I can't fund this project, so I'm afraid it's dead."

In one moment, everything we'd invested in, prayed about, and hoped for simply disappeared. As I put down the telephone, I felt sick and filled with one question: "God, why? Why have you led us this far only to let it be killed?"

Later that day, my pastor, Dwight Ham, met me and said, "I believe the Lord told me to give you this," and he handed me a cassette tape of a sermon by Derek Prince called, "The Grace of Yielding." At home all alone in my living room I began listening. Derek was teaching on God's test of Abraham's faith when he asks him to sacrifice his only son, Isaac. Derek described the experience of his first wife, Lydia, who had followed God's call to leave her home in Denmark to go to Jerusalem where she established a home for young girls orphaned in the growing violence between Arabs and Jews in the years leading up to Israel's formation as a nation in 1948. After a number of incredibly difficult years – and miraculous stories of God's intervention—a man began helping her as a volunteer. Gratefully, she accepted his help and developed trust in him. To her shock, he one day announced that he was taking over the ministry and no longer needed her services. Lydia was a tenacious fighter by nature, and she had no intention of just lying down and giving up. This was the ministry God had called her to and for which she had given her life. But God had a second surprise in store. As she cried out to God to restore the ministry to her, she heard the Lord direct her to the story of Abraham's call to sacrifice Isaac. Suddenly she realized that God had asked Abraham to walk out his trust in God by giving up the very thing God had promised him. And in the same way, God was now asking her to give up the very thing God had given her. She had to trust God instead of her rights over the ministry God had given her. She had to trust God instead of the incredible investments she had made in the promises of God for her ministry. And she did.

In her greatest step of faith she sacrificed her God-given ministry to the God who gave it to her in the first place. The rest of her life became something it could never have been had she held onto what she already had. She married Derek Prince, with him adopted eight of the Arab girls she had rescued from the streets, adopted a ninth daughter during a significant time of ministry in Kenya, and spent the rest of her life impacting the lives of thousands of people with healing and deliverance—including me. She never lost her incredible fighting spirit. She just knew when and to whom to submit.

There was much more to that sermon, and in it all I heard the whisper of God to me: lay down your Isaac. For at least five years, I had a card posted above my desk with this verse printed on it:

"In hope against hope Abraham believed...with respect to the Promise of God, he did not waver in unbelief but grew strong in faith, giving glory to God, and being fully assured that what God had promised, he was also able to perform...[for He] gives life to the dead, and calls into being that which does not exist." Romans 4:18, 20, 21, 17 NASB

Every day, I would read that verse and try to put my faith in God's promise to make our company succeed in its mission to bring the Gospel in powerfully creative ways to my generation. But on that day as I listened to "The Grace of Yielding", I was hearing about the kind of faith exhibited in Abraham's seventh test—the faith that lets the living promise die trusting in resurrection, that lets the something be wiped away trusting in what does not yet exist. This was clearly a much deeper kind of faith.

I felt as though what I was being asked to lay down was not simply the "ministry" of creating in music and media, but the kind of "faith" that would have held God accountable for leading me to this place—with visions, and words, and miraculous interventions—and then not coming through. I can still remember the layout of the room, the chair I was sitting in, the cold rain outside the windows, even the temperature. And I let go of my dreams and expectations, of the closely-held promises I believed God had made to me, of my life-long desire to create. And I wept for a very, very long time.

When I woke up the next morning, something had changed inside me. The day before, I had chosen to lay down my "ministry". Overnight, the desire that drove that ministry died. The best description I can give is to imagine Pablo Picasso waking up one morning to discover he no longer wants to paint, or John Lennon waking up to discover he doesn't ever want to write another song. I felt totally disoriented as a person wondering what now?

Looking back, it was that decision that ultimately freed me to hear God's call to become a pastor. The desire to create in media which died, God resurrected as a desire to create in teaching and preaching. And I am so thankful for all of it!

This seventh of Abraham's tests of faith is the last and most intense, but the sixth is at the heart of God's promises—for Abraham and for us—and it has to do with our authority to pray…If he hadn't passed the sixth test, he would never have been able to face the seventh.

(6) Genesis 18:17–18, 22–23
What will you do with unbelieving people who deserve and face judgment?

The story begins with these words, "The Lord appeared again to Abraham near the oak grove belonging to Mamre." How Abraham recognizes that one of the three men he suddenly sees standing near his tent is the Lord is never explained. But after allowing Abraham to prepare and serve a large meal, one of them renews the promise that Sarah will give birth to Abraham's long-awaited heir, "by about this time next year." Then the three set out from Abraham's home towards the city of Sodom. Here is the test:

The Lord says—either to himself or to his two companions—"'Should I hide my plan from Abraham?...For Abraham will certainly become a great and mighty nation, and all the nations of the earth will be blessed through him...' So the Lord told Abraham, 'I have heard a great outcry from Sodom and Gomorrah because their sin is so flagrant...'".

Think about God's reasoning: I am on my way to determine the facts of the case against Sodom and Gomorrah. Since Abraham is my choice to release blessing to all the nations, I will let him in on what I am doing to these nations. Will his heart, as my chosen partner, reflect mine? And will he take his responsibility seriously and *act*?

We hear the words "Sodom and Gomorrah" and immediately think of a society so saturated in sin that judgment is more than deserved and definitely overdue. Our thinking is: "God sees sin and brings judgment. Period." And so we miss the heart of God and the test of Abraham—and its implications for us as Abraham's promised descendants.

Look at God's words to Abraham in verses 20 and 21. "I have heard a great outcry from Sodom and

Gomorrah because their sin is so flagrant. I am going down to see if their actions are as wicked as I have heard. *If not, I want to know*" (my emphasis).

What is God telling Abraham he'd like to know? He'd like to know if there are any good things to balance against the bad *because his heart is not to execute judgment but to extend mercy.*

The test is to reveal what is in Abraham's heart. Think about it! God has promised Abraham that the land now occupied by other nations will one day belong to him. Here's an opportunity to see judgment remove at least a couple of those nations. God is giving Abraham three options:

Option #1—To stand on the side of judgment. "Lord, it's about time! Worse than you've heard. I've been wondering how long you'd wait. They deserve whatever judgment you bring and more."

Option #2—To say nothing. "Who am I to say anything about this one way or another. I mean, these aren't my people and it's not my business. Besides, you're God and I'm not. You're the one who hears and sees everything. My perspective is pretty limited. Do whatever you want."

Option #3—To assume the responsibility and act in the authority God's promise has conferred upon him—to *pray for mercy*. As the story reveals, this is the option Abraham seizes.

So much needs to be said about the mercy part of this test: how God's heart of mercy is over and over again displayed and described in the *Old* Testament (not just in the *New* Testament) and is at last fully incarnated in Jesus Christ. He states explicitly "Love your enemies! Do good to them...Then you will truly be acting as children of the Most High..." (Luke 6:35). And he lives out the heart of God's mercy on the cross where full judgment is executed on all sin and full pardon is extended to all who repent and embrace mercy.

Here, the point is simply this: God deliberately came to Abraham and told him of his plans for Sodom and Gomorrah. Why? Because he recognizes the authority he is giving Abraham for the fulfillment of the promise—to be the instrument of God's blessing to the nations. That authority is not one of conquest and control, but of praying for God's mercy and blessing.

We have the authority to pray for personal needs AND FOR NATIONS! Will we act on the responsibility God has entrusted to us?

CHAPTER 10

Or Are We Just Kidding Ourselves?

But let's get real— why pray for nations when nations don't appear to change in response to our prayer? Although the authority to pray for nations seems to be Biblical (if you've followed the argument of the previous chapter), nations don't appear to change in the right direction even though many are praying for those changes—at least in the experience of many of us.

In 1973, a widespread prayer movement was birthed and spread to hundreds of churches and thousands of sincere believers across America. On the first Friday of each month leading up to the 200th anniversary of the signing of this country's Constitution, people fasted and then gathered to pray for our nation. Spearheading this movement, Intercessors for America was formed—an organization with a broad reach that still champions prayer for our country. Yet, few would argue that today America is closer to God. Most of us would conclude the very opposite is true.

Is God actually calling us to pray for nations (and our local needs)? Do our prayers actually make a difference?

Before turning to some crucial Biblical passages, consider these three contemporary experiences.

In his book, *Shaping History Through Prayer and Fasting*, Derek Prince recounts an experience while he and his wife, Lydia, were serving as educational missionaries in Kenya from 1957 to 1961. Throughout much of Africa, colonial rule was being replaced by indigenous governments— but this was often accompanied by horrific internal strife. Kenya itself had suffered from years of a bloody insurgency called the Mau Mau movement, and would ultimately be given its independence from British rule in 1963. But in 1961, the outlook for a peaceful transition seemed dim.

In 1960, the neighboring Belgian Congo gained its independence and was immediately plunged into a series of inter-tribal conflicts—a legacy that still continues fifty years later. Many Europeans fled eastward into Kenya, bringing with them horrific accounts of the strife and chaos they had experienced.

This was the background against which political forecasts of Kenya's future were painted. And they were, as Derek recounts, "dark indeed."

In August of 1960, Derek was one of a number of missionaries gathered to minister at a week-long conference for about 200 African young people held in western Kenya. The final session was on Sunday where a missionary from Canada was giving the talk. His translator was Wilson Mamboleo, a young man recently graduated from the Teacher Training College of which Derek was the headmaster.

Derek vividly remembers the unusual events that unfolded:

> "The first two hours of the service followed a normal pattern, but after the close of the missionary's address, the Holy Spirit moved with sovereign power and lifted the meeting onto a supernatural plane. For the next two hours, almost the whole group of more than two hundred people continued in spontaneous worship and prayer without any visible human leadership.
>
> At a certain point, the conviction came to me that, as a group, we had touched God, and that His power was at our disposal. God spoke to my spirit and said, 'Do not let them make the same mistake that Pentecostals have so often made in the past, by squandering My power in spiritual self-indulgence. Tell them to pray for the future of Kenya.'
>
> Reaching the platform, I called the whole group to silence and presented God's challenge to them. 'You are the future leaders of your people,' I told them, 'both in the field of education and also in the field

of religion. The Bible places upon you, as Christians, the responsibility to pray for your country and its government. Your country is now facing the most critical period in its history. Let us unite together in praying for the future of Kenya.'

Wilson Mamboleo was with me on the platform, translating my words into Swahili. When the time came to pray, he knelt down beside me. As I led in prayer, almost every person present joined me in praying out loud…The sound of prayer swelled to a crescendo then suddenly ceased. It was as if some invisible conductor had brought down his baton.

After a few moments of silence, Wilson stood up and spoke to the congregation. 'I want to tell you what the Lord showed me while we were praying,' he said. I realized that God had given him a vision as he knelt beside me in prayer.

Wilson then related the vision he had seen, first in English and then in Swahili. 'I saw a red horse approaching Kenya from the east,' he said. 'It was very fierce, and there was a very black man riding on it. Behind it were several other horses, also red and fierce. While we were praying, I saw all the horses turn around and move away toward the north.'

Wilson paused for a moment, and then continued, 'I asked God to tell me the meaning of what I had seen, and this is what He told me: Only the supernatural power of the prayer of My people can turn away the troubles that are coming upon Kenya!'"

pp. 84–86

Looking back from this vantage point, it is remarkable to compare Wilson Mamboleo's vision with the subsequent history of Kenya and its neighbors. In his book, Derek outlines that amazing history:

"During the period of British rule, Kenya was one of three states that made up British East Africa. The other two states were Uganda to the west and

Tanganyika to the south (Tanganyika was later renamed Tanzania.) Kenya eventually achieved her independence on December 12, 1963. The other two states had already achieved independence somewhat earlier. Immediately after independence was declared, a national government was duly elected in Kenya, with Jomo Kenyatta as the nation's first president.

In January 1964, there was an exact outworking in Kenya's history of the vision that Wilson had seen. A bloody revolution broke out in Zanzibar, off Kenya's east coast. This was led by an African from Uganda who had been trained in revolutionary tactics under Castro in Cuba. The revolution succeeded in overthrowing the Sultan of Zanzibar.

In the same month, a revolutionary movement gripped the national army of Tanzania. Its influence also spread to the army of Kenya. The aim was to overthrow the elected government of Kenya and to replace it by a military dictatorship under communist control.

At this critical point, Kenya's new president, Jomo Kenyatta, acted with wisdom and firmness. Enlisting the help of the British army, he suppressed the revolutionary movement in the Kenyan army and restored law and order throughout the country. Thus, the authority of Kenya's duly-elected government was preserved, and the communist attempt at a military takeover was completely foiled.

In Wilson's vision, the red horses that turned away from Kenya moved towards the north. Northward along the African coast from Kenya lies Somalia. The kind of communist military coup that failed in Kenya was successful in Somalia. Someone later described Somalia as "a communist military camp."

The other countries bordering on Kenya have likewise experienced serious political problems. To the south, in Tanzania, strong communist influence has brought about various limitations of political freedom. To the west, in Uganda, there has been a history of unstable government and internal tribal clashes, with a very determined effort by the Moslems to gain control of the country and to make Islam the official religion of the nation. Yet in the midst of all this, Kenya has succeeded in combining order and progress with a high degree of political and religious liberty to a remarkable extent.

The attitude of Kenya's government toward Christianity has been consistently friendly and cooperative. Although President Kenyatta does not himself profess to be a Christian, he has officially invited the various Christian bodies in Kenya to teach the message of Christianity in every government school in the country. In many ways, Kenya has become a strategically located center from which trained national Christians are able to move out with the gospel message to all the surrounding countries.

Sometimes God uses unexpected means of getting information to us. In October, 1966, I was in the office of a travel agency in Copenhagen, making arrangements for a flight to London. While I was waiting for my ticket to be prepared, I picked up an English edition of the *London Times*. There was a special sixteen page supplement that dealt exclusively with Kenya. In essence, the theme of this supplement was that Kenya had proved to be one of the most stable and successful of nearly fifty new nations that had emerged on the continent of Africa since the end of World War II. As I turned each page of the supplement, I seemed to hear the inaudible voice of God within my spirit, saying, 'This is what I can do when Christians pray with faith for the government of their nation.'"

pp. 87–89

That occurred in the 1950's. Less than a decade later, John Sandford experienced something similar, which he describes in his book, *Healing The Nations—A Call To Global Intercession*.

One day in the early 1960's he had a vivid vision in which he found himself in front of an A-frame building. Together with another individual whom he knew well, he entered and proceeded through dark glass doors into a large room. There were rows of high-backed chairs, curved tables with benches at the front forming a circle and at its head, a large, straight table behind which sat the Lord—although they could not see him clearly. The entire row was occupied, except for one bench and table. In his own words:

> "Not a word was said, but we knew we were expected to be seated. The council was waiting for us to take our places before beginning.
>
> With no preamble the voice of God said, '*Shall we bomb?*'
>
> In those day's atomic warfare loomed on the horizon of most people's minds. My friend and I knew we were being asked, in the tremendous economy or words in such councils, whether the time had come to take drastic action. Should God let judgment fall, or would He extend mercy and more time?
>
> We thought a moment, then answered, 'No, please give the world more time.'
>
> Instantly the voice of God thundered, '*Do you know the cost of what you are asking?*'
>
> Visions of horrors cascaded through our minds. We saw many events that have since taken place and some that have not yet, though they still could: wars all over the earth; massacres as in Rwanda and Yugoslavia; millions of abortions; soaring crime rates; the corruption (and powerful lobby) of homosexuality; sexual immorality; bestiality; drugs and alcohol devouring many; marriages breaking up in divorce; children not raised in solid families crashing into all manner of evils.

> All this we saw in a moment. We knew the Lord was telling us that the longer judgment is withheld, the worse mankind will become. The mystery of lawlessness was already at work and increasing its grip on mankind year by year. But we also saw multitudes being saved and a great move of God coming.
>
> We meditated, consulted and finally responded, 'No, we don't know the cost of what we're asking. But we still plead for more time for mankind.'
>
> A decision was made. We were told to pray in repentance every day for an entire year, and to enlist others. Judgment would be withheld for a while.
>
> Not more than a few weeks later, the world teetered on the brink of nuclear war during the Cuban missile crises.
>
> Many others, I am sure, were called into prayers of repentance during that time. But I will never forget that dreadful council or the awesome weight of responsibility we felt."
>
> pp. 137–139

I hesitate to use this example because, although it so clearly demonstrates the partnership of God with us through prayer for changing the course of nations—it is so unusual and different than our normal experience. But, if you are thinking "Can I really believe this account?" consider these facts.

First, the kind of experience John recounts is a kind of experience recorded throughout the Bible. Whether you start at the back of the book with the Apostle John's spectacular series of visions in Revelation or Paul's brief mention of being "caught up to the third heaven" where he heard "inexpressible words which a man is not permitted to speak" (2 Corinthians 12:2–4). Or whether you start at the front of the book with Abraham's experience of being overcome with "a deep sleep and a terrific darkness" in which he hears the Lord's voice, and then sees "a smoking firepot and a flaming torch" pass between the sacrificed animals Abraham has arranged (Genesis 15:12–21), or Jacob's famous dream of the stairway to heaven with angels going up and down and the Lord standing at the top (Genesis 18:12–15). My point is that the Bible is filled front to back (or back to front) with these sorts of extraordinary experiences. We ought to recognize two things from the Biblical record: first, that God uses these means as a way of speaking to men and women, and second, that these occurrences are occasional and rare. (There is a "more normal" set of spiritual experiences that are meant to be very frequent—dreams and visions, words of wisdom and knowledge, prophecy and tongues with interpretation—see Paul's list in 1 Corinthians 12:14). What this means is that we should both expect that God will give some people a few of these very vivid, "supernatural" experiences, but we should not expect very many of them very often.

Second, each of these valid experiences will face the "scandal of particularity." That phrase captures the skeptical attitude towards anything that only happens once to one person in one place. It is the basis for dismissing the possibility that Jesus was born of a virgin (only once to one woman, Mary, in one place, Nazareth), was the incarnate Son of God, was crucified in Jerusalem for the sins of the whole world, and was raised from dead. The reality is, God regularly works in one person in one particular place in unique ways.

And, finally, accepting the reality of someone else's experience will depend upon the wider realities of that person's life. Are they a credible witness? I believe that in John Sandford's case we see a man whose life and ministry over many decades has born the good fruit of honesty, integrity and trustworthiness.

And so, I have chosen to include it as a contemporary revelation of how significant our prayers are for the course of nations.

Finally, let me recount a much more "normal" and frequent sort of event. On September 11, 2001, Stormie O'Martian experienced something that many, many more "ordinary" people who are committed to and faithful in prayer have also experienced. In her book, *The Power Of A Praying Nation*, she writes:

> "I woke up at 3:30 in the morning on September 11, 2001, with a deep feeling of dread, overwhelming sadness, and suffocating oppression. It was so heavy on me that it felt like the weight of the world. At first I thought something terrible must have happened or

> that someone had died. I'd awakened with a similar feeling several years before on the morning after the sudden tragic death of a close friend. Yet I don't even recall that feeling being as strong as what I was experiencing at this particular moment...I realized I needed to pray, but I didn't know exactly what to pray about..."

She then describes a series of prayer experiments. First, she prayed for her immediate family, then her extended family, then her friends. But none of these prayers seemed to hit the mark. After some time, she asked God, "Has something terrible happened that I don't know about? Is something bad *about* to happen? What is this heavy oppression, Lord?"

She continued to pray for various things as they came to mind, but she heard no clear answer or direction from God. At least a couple of hours passed before she finally fell asleep. She was still sleeping when her husband, Michael, burst into their bedroom and turned on the TV. "An airplane hit one of the World Trade Center towers, and as I was watching the news coverage, another plane ran right into the other tower. They are both on fire."

This is Stormie's description of what happened next:

> "At that moment, I remembered awakening in the middle of the night with the same terrible oppressive feeling. And suddenly I realized what that was all about. "Oh Lord, you were calling me to pray for our country, but I didn't get it," I said. I prayed for myself, and my loved ones, but I didn't think to pray for my country."

Stormie is not saying that had she prayed for our nation the attack on the World Trade Center and the Pentagon would have been averted. That is a question—let's face it—that none of us could ever answer. But what she *is* saying is that she believes God woke her up because he wanted to enlist her in praying *so that there would be a different outcome than there was without her prayer.* What sort of different outcome?

One of the most crucial insights we need to both partner effectively with God and fully trust him at every moment and in every circumstance, is to recognize that God is not an all or nothing God, nor are his plans all or nothing plans.

On the morning of September 11, 2001, a woman in my church was scheduled to fly to San Francisco on one of the airplanes that struck the World Trade Center. In fact, this had been a weekly routine for many months. On this particular Monday, however, she was asked by her daughter to stay home to care for her granddaughter. She debated about what she should do, and finally decided to delay her flight by a day.

I personally know of three people with similar stories that kept them off the hijacked planes or away from their office in the destroyed building on that fateful morning…and I live near Boston, not New York. Did God intervene to keep these people away because of prayers? Or was this simply God's personal sovereign mercy at work? Of course, we don't know in some "scientific" way: Here's all the data concerning those who prayed and why. Here's how God registered these prayers and responded.

Then how do we know?

One thing we can know with certainty is that, in both the Biblical revelation God has given us, and in the experiences of praying people down through history, God invites our prayers and tells us that he alters events in response. According to the Bible and everyday experience, prayer can *prevent* something from happening entirely. Pray can also *mitigate* the effects of what does happen.

On this side of heaven, we will never know how many terrible events have been averted in the life of our nation because of people's prayers—or how many good things have happened. We also will never know to what extent God has acted in the midst of terrible things to limit their extent and to protect the lives of many who would otherwise have been destroyed.

Prayer is always based on faith: acting on an "assurance about things we cannot see" (Hebrews 11:1). God is not all-or-nothing; his plans are not all-or-nothing. And our prayers are not all-or-nothing. That means that the effect of any one prayer can be greater or smaller. So how can our prayers have a greater effect? What can we do? I believe there are a handful of crucial—and very practical—factors.

One major factor in the effectiveness of our prayers is the condition of our hearts.

In one of God's encounters with Jeremiah, he tells him, "Even if Moses and Samuel stood before me pleading for these people, I would not help them" (Jeremiah 15:1). What does that tell us about the link between the *effectiveness* of prayer and the *character* or *heart condition* of the pray-er? God is singling out these two men because their prayers altered the course of the nation of Israel's history. Moses oversaw the birth of the nation as it was delivered from its slavery to Egypt into its freedom in the land of promise. Samuel presided over Israel's emergence from anarchy, where "all the people did whatever seemed right in their own eyes" (Judges 21:25), into the unity of the monarchy under David and Solomon. Their prayers were especially effective because each of them had a long history of *harmony with the heart of God.*

What I'm saying is that not only is God not an all-or-nothing God who carries out all-or-nothing plans, but in addition, we who pray are not all-or-nothing people whose prayers are totally effective or not effective at all. The truth is that we can grow in our effectiveness, or diminish. One key to growing in our effectiveness is growing in our personal harmony with the heart of God.

The Bible makes this very clear. For example, in Isaiah 58, God speaks to his people who are religiously observing God's command to fast and pray on specific days each year so that he can bless their nation—its productivity, its security, its overall health as a society. He describes what they're doing and the results they expect:

> "They act so pious! They come to the Temple every day and seem delighted to learn all about me. They act like a righteous nation that would never abandon the laws of its God. They ask me to take action on their behalf [*they are praying for their nation*] pretending they want to be near me [*genuinely wanting to know God's heart in order to be in harmony with his heart*]. 'We have fasted before you,' they say. 'Why aren't you impressed? We have been very hard on ourselves, and you don't even notice it!'"
>
> Isaiah 58:2–3a

To make sure we're getting the point: These are people who are praying for their nation. They are believers who are doing religiously correct things—going to the Temple (going to church), praying and even fasting. But their prayers are not effective. Why?

God continues:

> "I will tell you why!...
> It's because you are fasting to please yourselves.
> Even while you fast you keep oppressing your workers...you keep on fighting and quarreling..."
> Isaiah 58:3b–4

Then God tells us what would make our prayers effective:

> "Free those who are wrongly imprisoned; lighten the burden of those who work for you...remove the chains that bind people.
> Share your food with the hungry and give shelter to the homeless..."
>
> Isaiah58:6–7

The way to increase the effectiveness of prayer is to be in harmony with the heart of God. And harmony is learned, chosen, and lived out.

Another example is in Malachi where, again, God is speaking directly to his people who are complaining that their prayers for the nation are being ignored. God tells them why their prayers are ineffective:

> "You cover the Lord's altar with tears, weeping and groaning because he pays no attention to your offerings and doesn't accept them with pleasure. You cry out, 'Why doesn't the Lord accept my worship?' I'll tell you why! Because the Lord witnessed the vows you and your wife made when you were young. But you have been unfaithful to her, though she remained your faithful partner, the wife of your marriage vows...So guard your heart. Do not be unfaithful to your wife."
>
> Malachi 2:13–16

The effectiveness of our prayers is affected by how we live out our marriage relationship! This particular issue is reiterated in Peter's first letter in the New Testament where he writes:

> "...you husbands must give honor to your wives. Treat your wife with understanding as you live together. She may be weaker than you are, but she is your equal

partner in God's gift of new life. Treat her as you should *so your prayers will not be hindered."*

1 Peter 3:7, my emphasis

These three passages make a clear connection between the effectiveness of our prayers and the degree of harmony with the heart of God that we are living out. Praying is not a disconnected exercise; it is something that is fully integrated with our actual relationship with God. The bottom line of all prayer is, as Jesus told us, "Let your kingdom come, let your will be done on earth." We must want God's will in every aspect of our own lives before asking that it be done in the lives of others.

Again, this is not all-or-nothing! We are growing into greater harmony and more effectiveness, or falling back into disharmony and less effectiveness.

Just at this point, those of us who are most honest might be most discouraged from praying for anything. We might look at different places in our lives and recognize all the disharmony and feel all our faith drain from all our prayers. That is the voice of our Accuser, not our Advocate, who "pleads our case before the Father if anyone does sin." Our Advocate is Jesus Christ, the one who is truly righteous (1 John 2:1b). To be "truly righteous" is to be truly in harmony with the heart of God. The heart of God is for Jesus to plead our case: "I died according to your plan, Father, so that they would be forgiven for that sin and cleansed from all its ill effects" (1 John 1:9). The condition we have to fulfill is "to live in the light…and confess our sins" (1 John 1:7 and 9). The word for "confess" in the original Greek text is "homologeo"—a word which literally means "to say the same as". By saying the same thing about our action or attitude or words as God says about it (instead of justifying, excusing, denying, or deciding it's really okay), we are coming into harmony with God's heart.

This is why Jesus tells the story he does contrasting ineffective prayer with effective prayer (Luke 18:9–14). He describes two men who are praying in sight of each other. One is highly religious—a Pharisee. The other is a sinner—"a despised tax collector." The Pharisee tells God in prayer how good he is by recounting all the laws he *hasn't* broken (like cheating and adultery) and all the good religious things he does (like fasting twice a week and faithfully tithing). The tax collector prays by asking for mercy, saying "I am a sinner" and "beating his chest in sorrow."

It was this man's prayer that was effective, not the other's, because "those who exalt themselves will be humbled, and those who humble themselves will be exalted."

A significant element of effective prayer is personal authenticity before God, recognizing that he is fully aware of everything about us. And if we are personally authentic before God, our prayers *will* be effective.

Effectiveness increases as our lives are lived in harmony with God's heart. Effectiveness can begin every time we pray with openness and authenticity. The effectiveness of our prayers is not all-or-nothing. It is *increasing* or *decreasing*. To take prayer seriously—as God does—is to take our whole lives seriously—as God does.

The question we're wrestling with in this chapter is "Why pray for nations when nations don't appear to change in response to prayers?" The reason I am spending so much time on this is because it is one of the most significant barriers to long-term prayer. Many people get excited about the power of prayer, but lose motivation as time goes by and there seems to be no change as a result of their prayers. I know, because I have lost motivation to pray for apparently unchanging situations many, many times myself. Those times have pressed me to re-examine my foundations and re-think my expectations.

What I am sharing in this chapter are a handful of elements I have discovered that have helped me recover and deepen my faith in God's promise to respond to our prayers—and in fact to *not respond unless we pray*. These are things that have helped me embrace the Biblical revelation that there is *extreme significance* in whether God's people pray—and to learn to pray effectively.

One of those motivators is the record of contemporary examples of prayer for nations that resulted in change. I began with three different types of experiences.

A second motivator is the understanding that God's response to our prayers is not all-or-nothing. God might intervene to stop a nuclear holocaust (John Sandford's experiences), or to protect people in the midst of an unstopped tragedy (the experience of 9/11).

A third motivator is recognizing that the effectiveness of my prayer can increase (or decrease). If Moses were to pray for the same thing I am praying for, he would have greater success than I would because he was in greater harmony with God's heart than I am. Therefore, I want to engage in prayer with others. I want to listen to those who are more effective in prayer when they call for prayer for specific things. And I want to increase in my effectiveness by seeking to come into and live out harmony with the heart of God.

A fourth motivator is this: understanding that prayer is cumulative. We have already discovered that a person God singles out as an example for all of us of an effective pray-er is Elijah. As James put it succinctly: "The earnest prayer of a righteous person [one who is in harmony with the heart of God] has great power and produces wonderful results [has a high level of effectiveness]. Elijah was as human as we are, and yet when he prayed earnestly that no rain would fall, none fell for three and a half years! Then, when he prayed again, the sky sent down rain and the earth began to yield its crops" (James 5:16b-18).

We don't have a description of how Elijah prayed that no rain would fall, but we do have one for the rain's return. The story is found in 1 Kings, chapter 18. Elijah has just demonstrated God's supremacy over the demonic storm-god worshiped as Baal by the people and rulers of the Northern Kingdom of Israel. God has responded to Elijah's prayer by sending a fire which burns up not only the sacrificial bull laid out on pieces of wood atop a stone altar—the fire burns up the bull, the wood, the stones, the dust and the water Elijah has poured all over everything and that had filled a trench he'd dug around the whole ensemble.

"Then," the story reads, "Elijah said to Ahab [Israel's king], go get something to eat and drink, for I hear a mighty rainstorm coming!"

Although we have not been let in on how or when Elijah "heard" this rainstorm, it reveals that either at that moment or at some time before this Elijah had received some sort of audible impression he knew signified that God's intention was to cause the three and half year drought to end. What Elijah (our model of an effective pray-er) does with that information is what? He *prays*!

The very practical principle is this: any *revelation* God gives is normally an *invitation* to pray in harmony with that information and the heart of God. That may mean to pray that God *not* allow that to happen. This was John Sandford's prayer response to the information about an imminent nuclear attack. It was Abraham's prayer response to

God's revelation that he was going to bring judgment on Sodom. It was Moses' prayer response to God revealing an impending judgment on Israel (Exodus 32:9–14). It was Amos' prayer response to God's revelation of impending judgment on his nation (Amos 7:1–9).

That makes some sense. If something *might* happen that we hope *won't* happen, it is natural to pray and ask God to change that outcome. What makes less sense is that God's revelation of a *positive* outcome is just as much an invitation to pray. The Bible teaches us that God often waits to act *until we pray*. The revelation is something like this: "Here's what I'd like to do—what's in my heart right now to do...what do *you* think?"

And the story makes an even more significant point regarding effective prayer:

> "So Ahab went up to eat and drink. But Elijah climbed to the top of Mount Carmel and bowed low to the ground and prayed with his face between his knees."

Recall the way James described prayer that is effective. He wrote, "the *earnest* prayer of a righteous person." A good way to describe earnest prayer would be "intense heartfelt prayer," or "focused heart-engaged prayer." Elijah's whole body demonstrates what it means to be earnest. He stoops down and puts his face between his knees. In that culture—as in many others around the world—this is the birthing position. Elijah is praying with such earnestness that he puts his whole body into the position of a woman in labor about to give birth. Effectiveness and heart-intensity are intimately linked. And doesn't that make perfect sense? It is reflected in Jesus' story of the man who beats his chest as he prays for mercy. It is reflected in Jesus' own reputation as a pray-er described in Hebrews: "he offered prayers and pleadings with a loud cry and tears" (Hebrews 5:7).

Here in Elijah's story, we don't know whether he prayed loudly, softly, or even silently. All we know is that the posture of his body reflected the intense earnestness of his heart as he prayed for what God had promised by revelation.

Effective prayer has to do with how much we really *care*. Increasing in our harmony with God's heart (how much do you think he *cares* about the situation—for which you are praying?), will increase our effectiveness.

This will *look* and *sound* differently for different people. I have a 100% Swedish heritage and am a convinced introvert. But my outward demeanor covers the degree of intensity in my heart. The person beside me when our team scores the winning touchdown goes crazy—jumping up and down, pumping his fist, shouting at the top of his lungs. He is Italian by heritage and is a gregarious extrovert. Just don't make the mistake of deciding that my "YES!", barely audible next to my shouting friend, demonstrates that my heart intensity is that much less than his. Because that would not be true. Someone can shout their prayers and have zero heart intensity. Someone else can whisper and have a heart intensity that is white-hot.

Another myth that needs debunking is that intensity is measured by emotion. Emotion can be stirred up by events; but intensity is determined by a commitment of will. I can *decide* whether and how much to be intensely caring about the object of my prayers.

There is one other practical principle of effective prayer demonstrated in this story: After bending down in the "labor" position to pray:

> "Then he said to his servant, 'Go and look out toward the sea.'
> The servant went and looked, then returned to Elijah and said 'I don't see anything.'
> *Seven times* Elijah told him to go and look.
> Finally the seventh time his servant told him, 'I saw a little cloud about the size of a man's hand rising from the sea.'
> Then Elijah said, 'Hurry to Ahab and tell him, 'Climb into your chariot and go back home. If you don't hurry, the rain will stop you!'
> And soon the sky was black with clouds. A heavy wind brought a terrific rainstorm."
>
> 1 Kings 18:43–45, my emphasis

Not only did Elijah receive God's revelation about an imminent end to the three and a half year drought as an invitation to pray, instead of passively waiting for God to fulfill it. Not only did Elijah pray *in earnest*—with tremendous heart intensity, Elijah also prayed over and over again (seven times) until he saw the fulfillment actually beginning. Why?

Because Elijah knew that effective prayer is *cumulative*. Many prayers have more weight than one prayer.

In many places throughout India, or Tibet, or Nepal people have set up "prayer flags" or immense "prayer wheels". The idea behind these is that each time the wind causes the flags to flap, or at every turn of the wheel the inscribed prayers are sent to the gods. In Catholic tradition, the Rosary beads perform a similar function. Is this what "cumulative prayer" looks like?

Of course not. These "prayers" are what Jesus described as "meaningless repetitions" (Matthew 6:7). Here are his actual words, "When you pray, don't babble on and on as people of other religions do. They think their prayers are answered merely by repeating their words again and again."

What is the difference between meaningless—therefore *ineffective*—prayers and *many* prayers which increase in their effectiveness as they increase in number?

Imagine you are praying the words Jesus next gives us in his instructions about how to pray effectively—and how to not pray ineffectively. These are the words we commonly call "The Lord's Prayer", or "The Our Father". Imagine as you finish the prayer I ask you this question: "What are you hoping to see if God answers that prayer?" What would you say?

If you say, "Well, I hope he'll bless me because I've prayed The Lord's Prayer", then you have just uttered a "meaningless repetition".

But if instead you say "I'm looking for God to heal my wife's cancer. I'm looking for a change in my boss's attitude towards me. I'm looking for help today in seeing victory over my tendency to become angry at my kids. I'm asking for forgiveness for treating my co-workers with contempt yesterday." Then, I would encourage you to use the words as Jesus intended them: as a pattern to guide us into effective praying: "My friend, knowing that God is our Father who loves us, and knowing that we are meant to pray for his kingdom (his active rule) to come and his will to be done here on earth in the same way it is carried out in heaven, pray for your wife's healing, pray for your relationship with your boss (listening for God's whisper about anything *you* may need to change or do), pray for his transforming power to change your heart, repenting of your anger and calling for blessing on your children by name…" You get the idea!

Effective prayer is always aimed at a specific purpose. Ineffective prayer is hoping for "points" in God's "book of fine religious deeds."

Prayers—genuine and effective prayers—*do* have a cumulative weight, however. And Elijah's story is not the only window into this reality.

The Apostle John sees a series of visions that connect the realms of heaven, peopled by angles and angelic beings, with earth's history represented not only by human beings but by grotesque beasts and unimaginable creatures symbolizing nations, rulers, and governmental forces. The record of those visions, the New Testament book titled "Revelation," is notoriously difficult to interpret and apply. As great a Biblical scholar as John Calvin wrote a commentary on every book of the Bible—except for Revelation. The giant of church history, Martin Luther, instructed his students and pastors to preach on every book of the Bible—but *not* on Revelation.

While agreeing that to interpret correctly and apply the whole of Revelation is beyond my ability, there are many parts of that whole that have had a tremendous impact on my life—and my praying. One of them is this:

> "When the Lamb broke the seventh seal on the scroll, there was silence throughout heaven for about half an hour. I saw the seven angels who stand before God, and they were given seven trumpets. Then another angel with a gold incense burner came and stood at the altar. And a great amount of incense was given to him to mix with the prayers of God's people as an offering on the gold altar before the throne. The smoke of the incense, mixed with the prayers of God's holy people, ascended up to God from the altar where the angel had poured them out. Then the angel filled the incense burner with fire from the altar and threw it down upon the earth; and thunder crashed, lightening flashed, and there was a terrible earthquake."
>
> Revelation 8:1–5

Like most visions, what John is seeing is a picture made up of symbols which stand for something. A vision also most often is aimed at communicating a single overarching point. The many details contribute to that main point.

What is the main point of this vision given to John? That our *cumulative prayers* will absolutely turn out to be effective! Our prayers—each and every one of them—have been carefully stored in heaven so that their fulfillment can be released at the right time.

This vision is a part of the much larger book of Revelation woven from the strands of many visions. They are enigmatically overlapping, not chronologically sequential—although there is an historical beginning point and an end point. The visions (the "revelation," or more literally, the "opening of the heavenly dimension" to John's earthly eyes and ears) begin with the Lion/Lamb-who-was-slain taking from God's hand a scroll symbolizing the Title Deed to earth and humanity. The visions, therefore, have an historical beginning point in 30AD at the Death-Burial-Resurrection-Ascension of Jesus Christ. The visions end with the descent of the Heavenly Jerusalem, establishing the final and permanent dwelling of God and the Lamb on earth—now "resurrected" from its "groaning-because-subjected-to-futility condition" (Romans 8:20–22) and transformed into the "new heavens and new earth" (Revelation 21:1). The visions, therefore, have an historical endpoint. We just don't know the date on the calendar—but there will be one.

As a whole, the book of Revelation tells the story of the Kingdom rule of God, which was inaugurated in the ministry of Jesus Christ, taking full effect. And in this particular telling of that story, which includes events past, present, and future, God is revealing a few important things. One is that the number of people who are saved and made into an eternal kingdom of priests for God is "too great to count" and includes people "from every nation and tribe and people and language" (Revelation 7:9). As the church, God is giving us a foundation for faith in the power of the Gospel. Many, many, many will be saved, not a few. Why not many in our neighborhoods and communities and places of work? Why not many in our nation?

A second important revelation in these woven visions is that God has a powerful, persistent, deceitful Enemy who will rally many rulers and nations to live lives flaunting the laws of God and finally to join a war against Jesus Christ when he returns to this earth to establish the governmental rule of God. Practically, this is a gut-check and a call to expect and endure suffering and persecution in the fulfillment of our commission to share the Gospel. Be encouraged: *many* will be saved. Do not be discouraged: many will reject you and your message. God is calling us to a battle—which *ends* in a banquet. He is calling us to *"overcome"* (Revelation 2:7, 11, 17, 26; 3:5, 12, 21 and 21:7).

A third hugely important revelation conveyed in the visions that make up the story of this book is that heaven and earth are intimately and continuously connected. Events on earth are important to heaven, and heaven is affecting events on earth. Angels are conveying information and carrying out a whole list of God's just judgments that impact the earth—from hailstorms and earthquakes to unmanned agents that pollute large areas of water resources and others that cause terrific bodily pain.

It is in the context of these three things—many, many being saved, many others rejecting salvation, and the revelation that earth and heaven are intimately and continually connected as God's Kingdom rule is being established in its fullness on earth as in heaven, that John records the vision of incense, prayer, and fire being thrown down to the earth.

Here is John's succinct description:

> "Then another angel with a gold incense burner came and stood at the altar. And a great amount of incense was given to him to mix with the prayers of God's people as an offering on the gold altar before the throne. The smoke of the incense, mixed with the prayers of God's holy people, ascended up to God from the altar where the angel had poured them out. Then the angel filled the incense burner with fire from the altar and threw it down upon the earth; and thunder crashed, lightening flashed, and there was a terrible earthquake."
>
> Revelation 8:3–5, my emphasis

The crucial point of this vision is that our prayers *from* earth are instrumental in releasing heaven's power *to* earth. But it's not a one-to-one immediate transaction. Many prayers have been received and preserved until God determines the appropriate time of that fulfillment.

And notice the awesome promise that *incense is added* to our prayers! Throughout the Bible incense is used as a symbol of prayer. So here, heaven's incense is added to earth's incense—heaven's prayers are added to ours. This simply reinforces what Paul told us: that the Holy Spirit "helps us in our weakness...[and] prays for us with groaning that cannot be expressed in words...in harmony with God's own will (Romans 8:26–27).

Sometimes, we read that as a purely personal matter: the Holy Spirit will be praying for God to do certain things in an individual's own heart and life. I would suggest that while those things are *included*, there is a far wider scope to these prayers.

The context of this praying is "the glory [God] will reveal" for which "all creation is waiting eagerly" (Romans 8:18ff). It is the final culmination of the inbreaking Kingdom of God, the transformation of all things. And at every moment each of us is involved in the ongoing process which will culminate in that event. Every effective prayer is for the inbreaking Kingdom of God—God's will being done on earth. Every prayer, no matter how weak and seemingly insignificant and as yet unanswered, is received and preserved in heaven, and to it is added the prayers of the Holy Spirit, and of Jesus Himself, who "lives forever *to intercede with God on [our] behalf*" (Hebrews 7:25b).

What an encouragement to pray in expectation of God's answer—whether for personal needs or for nations. God keeps encouraging us to realize the incredible power of our prayers—though they seem so weak and unanswered.

> "I strongly suspect that if we saw all the differences even the tiniest of our prayers make, and all the people those little prayers were destined to affect, and all the consequences of those prayers down through the centuries, we would be so paralyzed with awe at the power of prayer that we would be unable to get up off our knees for the rest of our lives."
> -Peter Kreeft, professor of Philosophy, Boston College

Or at least, we'd be strikingly more committed to praying every day and about every thing.

CHAPTER 11

Praying That Works

In this final chapter I want to share a very simple but very powerful tool to use for effective praying: the Word of God.

The great English Puritan, John Owens, once wrote: "The Scriptures are like a river so shallow a mouse can ford it, but so deep an elephant can bathe in it." Praying the Word does not require knowing much of the Word at all, but knowing much of the Word will expand your ability to use it powerfully in prayer.

I had been a Christian for many years before I heard someone teach on this subject. I'm sure I had many times quoted a verse of Scripture during one of my prayers; and I'm sure I'd heard others do it. But until I heard someone explain the value and power of using Scripture as a tool or prayer, I never understood its power. Therefore, I rarely used it. The tool rarely left my tool box. Perhaps that's been your experience.

Let's examine the tool, its powerful purpose in prayer, and how to develop increasing skill in using it.

There were two vital experiences that launched Jesus' Messianic ministry. The first was his baptism followed by receiving the Holy Spirit. The second was his forty-day fast in the wilderness followed by a personal encounter with Satan. In that encounter, Jesus was faced with and successfully overcame three temptations to step out of God's will and, along with Adam and the rest of the human race, fall short of the glory of God. Instead, (and in our stead), he was victorious.

What is recorded for us as significant was not simply *that* Jesus overcame each temptation, but *how* he did it. In all three cases—not merely one of them, or two—Jesus defended himself by using the Word of God. "The Scriptures say, "People do not live by bread alone, but by every word that comes from the mouth of God'" (quoting Deuteronomy 8:3). "The Scriptures say, 'You must not test the Lord your God'" (quoting Deuteronomy 6:16). "The Scriptures say, "You must worship the Lord your God and serve only him" (quoting Deuteronomy 6:13).

Why? Why didn't Jesus merely counter Satan's temptations with his own words? What did Jesus know that it might be worth *us* knowing?

Behind Jesus' use of the Scripture to confront Satan is an understanding of *what* Scripture is that makes it so powerful. First, the Word of God has power *because it is true.* Imagine a court case. Arguments are made. Evidence is presented. Witnesses are questioned. What is it that trumps everything? The *truth.*

In any human court, truth can be obscured and unrecognized. But God's Word is truth revealed.

That doesn't prevent us from misusing it. In fact Satan in this encounter with Jesus does just that, inciting Jesus to jump from the highest point on the Temple because "the Scriptures say, 'He will order his angels to protect you...'" (quoting from Psalm 91:11-12). There is a vast difference between using a gun to hit the bulls-eye and using it to shoot out someone's porch light. The point is that the Word of God is the truth and has the power of truth—when aimed correctly. It's not a toy gun; and it's not a fake gun.

Jesus also understood that the Word of God has power because it is God's own selection from what *might* have been written because these particular words apply to every generation throughout all history.

A lot of attention has been given to the authorial intent of each book in the Bible. An easy place to see this is John's Gospel when he writes "The disciples saw Jesus do many other miraculous signs in addition to the ones in this book. But these are written so that you may continue to believe that Jesus is the Messiah, the Son of God..." (John 20:31). To this he adds these closing words, "Jesus also did many other things. If they were all written down, I suppose the whole world could not contain the books that would be written" (John 21:25). John, as every other biblical author, has a purpose in mind for writing the book. That purpose determined his selection of events and how they are described.

Behind the author of each biblical book stands another, greater Author. He has an overarching purpose in which each individual book plays a part. And under his inspiration, the selection of words each author makes conforms to the selection the Author is making through and with them. The end product has power because it is intended to be used and applied by every generation.

In the famous set of teachings we call "The Beatitudes," Jesus says that he has not come to dismiss, abrogate, or alter the writings of Moses or the prophets (the entire written Old Testament). In fact, just the opposite is true: "I came to accomplish their purpose." Then he explains his understanding of the power of this selection of words that make up these writings: "I tell you the truth, until heaven and earth disappear not even the smallest detail of God's law will disappear until its purpose is achieved (Matthew 5:17-18). The actual words Jesus uses, here translated as "the smallest detail," are "jot and tittle." They refer to the tiniest strokes of the pen to write the Hebrew alphabet. This is how finely and carefully the selection of Scripture's words in truth are!

And Jesus himself used that selection with that understanding. For example, when asked for proof of a coming resurrection of the dead by the Jewish sect that taught there would be none, Jesus asked them:

> "Haven't you ever read about this in the Scriptures? Long after Abraham, Isaac, and Jacob had died, God said, "I am the God of Abraham, the God of Isaac, and the God of Jacob. So he is God of the living, not the dead."
>
> Matthew 22:31–32

Then another group of leaders opposed to the first group tried to trap him in a different argument. After responding to their question, he asks them his own question:

> "What do you think about the Messiah?
> Whose son is he?'
> They replied, 'He is the son of David.'
> Jesus responded, 'Then why does David, speaking under the inspiration of the Spirit, call the Messiah My Lord?' For David said, 'The Lord said to my lord, sit in the place of honor at my right hand until I humble your enemies beneath your feet.' Since David

called the Messiah, 'My Lord,' how can the Messiah be his son?'"

Matthew 22:41–45

Both of these arguments rely on a single word! In the first instance, it is the first-person verb "I am". In the second, it is the single word "Lord". Jesus relied on the care of God's selection process. And so he says to them: "Your mistake is you don't know the Scriptures, and you don't know the power of God" (Matthew 22:29). Knowing and understanding the Scriptures allows us to use them in prayer, relying on God's power to accomplish their purpose.

Jesus also understood the Word of God has power because it is living and powerful, as the writer of Hebrews describes it (Hebrews 4:12). Over and over again this living, active power of God's Word is described:

"…the entire universe was formed by the word of God."

Hebrews 11:3

"'Does not my word burn like fire?' says the Lord. 'Is it not like a mighty hammer that smashed a rock to pieces?'"

Jeremiah 23:29

"The rain and snow come down from the heavens and stay on the ground to water the earth. They cause the grain to grow, producing seed for the farmer and bread for the hungry. It is the same with my word. I send it out, and it always produces fruit. It will accomplish all I want it to, and it will prosper everywhere I send it."

Isaiah 55:10–11

Praying the Word of God—using the very words of Scripture in our prayer—increases the power and effectiveness of our prayer because it conveys the will of God. Effective prayer always invites God to carry out his will. His word is his own revelation to us of what his will is.

Suppose I am an alcoholic. I pray, "O God, please give me enough money to buy a drink." This will never be an effective prayer. Why not? Because the word of God states: "Flee drunkenness!"

God's will in this situation will emphasize, demonstrate, glorify, extend, and amplify God's will revealed in his word.

Effective prayer will always emphasize, demonstrate, glorify, extend, and will always amplify God's will revealed in his word.

There are two Biblical pictures that further uncover how essential our knowledge and use of God's word is in prayer to release God's heavenly will and power into our earth. The first is when Paul reminds us about the geography in which we live: it is a vast battlefield. Our enemies are not the people we see, but the panoply of beings we can't see: "evil rulers and authorities of the unseen world, mighty powers in this dark world, evil spirits in the heavenly places" (Ephesians 6:12). Our only choice is whether we will put up a good fight, or be taken down without a struggle. Will we be Jacob and Israel, or Esau? Or, as Paul writes, will we choose to "be strong in the Lord and in his mighty power" (Ephesians 6:10)? How can we become increasingly strong in the Lord? By putting on what Paul describes as God's armor: truth, God's ways of righteousness, trusting fully in—actually walking, putting all our weight on—God's grace/salvation, and answering every temptation to fear with the faith that trusts God's goodness all the time. Then Paul describes one final piece of the armor. It isn't exactly part of a soldier's armor; it is the one offensive weapon he has to take the battle to the enemy. It is, Paul says, "the sword of the Spirit, *which is the word of God*" (Ephesians 6:13–17).

To use the word of God in our prayers is to use words which have the power to cut into every enemy. That word is invested with the power of the Holy Spirit, himself. He inspired it. He made the careful selections. He knows its purpose and carries it out with his divine power.

A sword is an awesome thing. But it must be taken out of its sheath—that is, we must have lifted it from the whole of the Bible—and then wielded against a specific enemy—that is spoken against or into a specific situation.

The book of Psalms ends with a song that repeats these two words: "Praise him…" The last two lines are "Let everything that breathes sing praises to the Lord! Praise the Lord!" (Psalm 150:6). John sees a vision of its fulfillment, and he hears "every creature under heaven and on earth and under the earth and in the sea. They sang, "Blessing and honor and glory and power belong to the one sitting on the throne and to the Lamb forever and ever'" (Revelation 5:13). The Psalm is the instruction given in hope. It is the promise in anticipation. The scene in Revelation is the fulfillment.

But between promise and fulfillment lies a great gulf. The first does not and will not suddenly become the last.

I believe the next-to-last psalm pictures the mechanism of fulfillment:

> "The Lord delights in his people; he crowns the humble with victory. Let the faithful rejoice that he honors them. Let them sing for joy as they lie on their beds. Let the praises of God be in their mouths, and a sharp sword in their hands—to execute vengeance on the nations and punishment on the peoples, to bind their kings with shackles and their leaders with iron chains, to execute the judgment written against them. This is the glorious privilege of his faithful ones. Praise the Lord!"
>
> Psalm 149:4–9

What is the picture and what does it mean?

Clearly, the end result is the full and final reign of God over all the earth, every nation, and every king. Who brings this about? It is God, but through his people who are described as humble, faithful, and lying on their beds with a sharp sword in their hands.

In the much later light of Paul's battle instructions, we can more fully understand the Psalm's kings and leaders as the evil rulers of the unseen world who stand behind those who are seen. And, while the battle is certainly fought out in the open—sharing the Gospel, healing the sick, caring for the poor—it is also fought *on our beds*—a place behind the scenes where we use the sword of God's word in prayer and are *granted victory.*

Why give so much space to all these passages of Scripture? Because we need the abiding conviction that praying the word of God is using the word as a weapon of power crafted and forged by God himself meant for our use and his victory.

Let me end in a practical way by reviewing three biblical examples of people who prayed the word. How did they use the word of God in their prayers? What can we learn and apply in our own praying?

Of all the examples given in Scripture, Daniel is certainly one of the great pray-ers. Even when it meant arrest and being put to death, he prayed "with his windows open…three times a day just as he had always done" (Daniel 6:10). Prayer was a long-term, consistent, and results-oriented part of his life. One of his prayers is recorded at some length; and it is a practical model of using the word to pray. First Daniel tells us the background, then he shares what he prayed.

> "During the first year of his reign, I, Daniel, learned from reading the word of the Lord, as revealed to Jeremiah the prophet, that Jerusalem must lie desolate for seventy years. So I turned to the Lord God and pleaded with him in prayer and fasting…'O Lord, you are a great and awesome God! You always fulfill your covenant and keep your promises of unfailing love to those who love you and obey your commands. But we have sinned and done wrong…'"
>
> Daniel 9:2–5a

Daniel is praying because of and in accordance with the Word of God which he read in the book of Jeremiah. He focuses on the promise God had made to limit the exile of the Jewish people from the land of Israel and Jerusalem to seventy years. But his prayer is not simply: "God, your word says that you will bring us back to our land after seventy years. So do it!" No. He constructs a long argument based on God's character, past history, and present promises. He also describes the character, history, and present condition of himself and his people. All this is done with a very specific result in view: restoration to Israel and God's glory in the earth. And the prayer keeps elaborating, exploring, explaining, and therefore broadening and deepening Daniel's grasp of who God is, who we are, and why this particular request should be granted. Such praying magnifies God, humbles and aligns us with God and his ways, and measures the intensity of our commitment and longing to see his will done in the situation for which we are praying.

If you read Daniel's prayer as recorded, it will take you about three minutes. As with most recorded prayers, conversations, or sermons in Scripture, we are not reading the entire verbalization of what was said, but only a condensed version. Daniel's recorded prayer is demonstrating what he was saying for a lot longer time. And Daniel adds: "I went on praying, and confessing my sin and the sin of my people, pleading with the Lord my God for Jerusalem, his holy mountain" (Daniel 9:20).

Practically, praying the word uses the words of Scripture as a launching pad and focus for prayer. It does not simply quote the word and stop!

David is another great pray-er some of whose prayers are recorded. One of them is found in 2 Samuel,chapter 7. The prayer goes on for many verses, and then David says this:

> "O Lord of Heaven's Armies, God of Israel, I have been bold enough to pray this prayer to you because you have revealed all this to your servant, saying, 'I will build a house for you—a dynasty of kings.'"
>
> 2 Samuel 7:27

David could pray what he prayed for because he had God's word of revelation concerning God's will. David did not simply quote the words; he used them as the basis on which he constructed his prayer-arguments asking God to do what he promised. Praying the word is quoting God's own words back to him, and then amplifying and applying those words to the situation we are praying for.

One great way to learn this, and to discover the power of God's word to align us more and more to his character and his will, is to pray the Psalms. Each one was written with the intent of using them as prayers to God. Each day, take one psalm and pray it line by line, or phrase by phrase. Here's what is might look like on day one.

Psalm 1 begins: "Oh, the joys of those who do not follow the advice of the wicked, or stand around with sinners, or join in with mockers."

I begin by reading those words out loud—as a prayer before God's throne. I recognize that I am standing before the one who authorized those words, and with me in mind.

Then I will begin to amplify and apply those words:

> O Lord, I know how true it is that *joy* comes from doing things your way, and not from following the advice of those who *don't* like your ways. I don't want to listen to their advice…and, Lord, I am sorry for the times I have chosen their advice over yours. [Plenty of times, the Holy Spirit will call to mind things we need

to confess and repent of…if we are genuinely *praying* with earnest humility and openness.] And, Lord, I don't want to just hang out with sinners. I want to spend time with them like you did, Jesus…but not to get caught up with their behaviors. [Your elaboration will express your particular life journey.]

I believe you begin to get the idea! It is a deliberate process that leads to effective, transforming prayer. It is useful in both personal prayer and when praying as a group.

I have one last practical suggestion. As I read the Bible devotionally, I have two notebooks or journals with me. In one, I write out any verse or passage that particularly strikes me with relevance to my life. I will create a "title" for the passage that capsulizes the particular point that has impacted me.

For example, in reading Paul's instructions about giving in 2 Corinthians, he writes: "And don't give reluctantly or in response to pressure. 'For God loves a person who gives cheerfully'" (2 Corinthians 9:7). On this particular day, what strikes me are the words "God loves." If I give cheerfully, I am making God's heart swell with love. I determine to *choose* to give cheerfully every time I give. Every week as I write my tithe check, I determine to *be cheerful*. I want that attitude to accompany all my giving. And so, I write the following title in my notebook: *Giving Cheerfully Always Expands God's Heart With Love*. Then below the title I write out the actual words of the text. Doing that is a form of meditating on God's word, and in the process of titling and writing the Holy Spirit will often expand my understanding and application.

The second notebook is my Prayer Journal. In it, I do the same thing as I just described, but in this case I record verses of scripture that, when I read them, I want to *pray*. As an example, I might use the very same passage from 2 Corinthians for my Prayer Journal. In this notebook, instead of a title, I write the date, then below it, the scriptural passage.

Here's how I use that Journal. During my time of personal prayer, I will take some time to pray one or two of the scriptures I've recorded there. I normally don't single one out, but simply cycle through my list at the rate of one or two each day. It that were today's scripture, I might pray like this:

> O Father, everything I have and all the money I "make' comes from you as a gift. I am so sorry for the times when I am reluctant to give [if some instance comes to mind, I will confess and repent.] I want to be cheerful! It is a privilege to give to your work in the earth…

You get the idea! And the idea is to unite God's own carefully selected words as the basis for our prayer.

Irene Webster-Smith was one of the most fruitful missionaries to Japan. Among her many endeavors was the founding of an orphanage for Japanese girls, every one of whom she led to Christ.

One evening during their devotions, they read Mark 11:22-24, where Jesus said: "Have faith in God…I tell you the truth, if anyone says to this mountain, 'Go, throw yourself into the sea,' and does not doubt in his heart, but believes that what he says will happen, it will be done for him. Therefore I tell you, whatever you ask for in prayer, believe that you have received it, and it will be yours."

One little girl asked, "Sensei (Teacher), did Jesus really mean what He said?"

Irene Webster-Smith answered, "Of course, He meant what He said. Why do you ask?"

The child went on to say, "There is a large mountain between our Sunrise Orphanage and the Sea of Japan. If this were removed and cast into the sea, we would have a beautiful view of the ocean."

This was too much for Irene Webster-Smith's faith. She tried to soften the blow of disappointment by telling the little girl that Jesus did not necessarily mean a physical mountain, but rather that if we had problems in our lives and asked Him to remove them, He could. However, the child added, "But Sensei, Jesus said that if you say to this mountain. He was talking about a real one. I'm going to ask Him to take it away."

Not long after, they noticed there were bulldozers on the top of that mountain. When Irene asked the workers what they were doing, they told her that the Japanese Government had decided to use it for fill. So they were going to transport it all and throw it into the shallow part of the sea, in order to reclaim the land.

The little girl's prayer was literally answered! And the Sunrise Orphanage had a beautiful view of the Sea of Japan (J. Christy Wilson, *More to Be Desired Than Gold*, pp. 77–78).

The words of God are words God in heaven longs to fulfill. He only waits for his partners on earth to ask. Will you be one of those God *needs* to pray in order that his will may be done on earth? One of those who will learn his secrets of effective prayer that works? On the last page of my Bible I have written this Want Ad:

WANTED:

Willing learners—
 move mountains
  affect the course of nations
   direct line open at all times to the King of Kings
    benefits and pension plan include:
     things no eye has seen
      no ear has heard
       and no man has ever imagined...

FINAL VISION: UNITED TO JESUS

The High Priest

I want to share one final vision for prayer. I began with this goal: that from the insights and experiences contained in this book each of us and all of us would embrace prayer in deeper, more fulfilling and persistent ways. From God's perspective we not only carry the names "House of Prayer" and "Israel—wrestling with God and men so as to prevail," we also have been incorporated into the person of his Son, Jesus. We *are* the Body of Christ *on earth*. What does that mean for prayer?

Jesus Christ is not only the Savior and not only the King of Kings. He is—not just was—the faithful High Priest.

In laying out the organizational structure of His chosen people, God devotes considerable detailed attention to the clothing to be worn by the high priest. Behind these details lie God's intent to reveal the essential role of the high priest in the unfolding of his salvation for his people, and ultimately for the world. And prayer is at its very center.

Aaron, Moses' brother, was the first high priest and Israel was God's first people. But each represented and pointed forward to the ultimate fulfillment of God's promise to Abraham that through him *all* the families of the earth would be blessed (Genesis 12:3).

Israel was intended to be a light to all the nations, and at the same time, a representation of all the nations.

When Moses gives his final charge to the people he has led for over forty years, he reveals something about the *representative role* that God has created Israel to have:

> "When the Most High assigned lands to the nations,
> when he divided up the human race, he established

the boundaries of the peoples according to the number of the sons of Israel."

> Deuteronomy 32:8, NLT margin
> according to the Hebrew Masoretic Text)

On many occasions, the number which represents the whole of Israel is the number 70. For example, the book of Exodus—the book that begins the history of Israel, the nation, transitioning from Israel, the family of Abraham, Isaac, and Jacob—begins:

> "These are the names of the sons of Israel...In all, Jacob had seventy descendants in Egypt including Joseph, who was already there."
>
> Exodus 1:1–5

When God first gives Moses the Ten Commandments, he tells Moses to come further up the mountain of Sinai, and to "bring along Aaron, Nadab, Abihu, and seventy of Israel's elders (Exodus 24:1). In Numbers, God instructs Moses to gather "seventy men who are recognized as elders and leaders of Israel" (Numbers 11:16). Centuries later, when God shows Ezekiel a picture of his Temple being profaned, Ezekiel enters through a hidden doorway and sees "seventy leaders [burning] incense... to various idols (Ezekiel 8:9–11).

That number seventy is the number that Jewish Rabbinic tradition has always taken to represent all the Gentile nations. It is the number first given in Genesis 10 when all the descendants from Noah's three sons are given. After listing the seventy names, the account reads:

> "These are the clans that descended from Noah's sons, arranged by nation according to their lines of descent. *All nations of the earth descended from these clans* after the great flood."
>
> Genesis 10:32, my emphasis

When Jesus, therefore, sends out seventy of his disciples—not only the Twelve—he is deliberately making a prophetic declaration: that *all* God's people will be carrying this message of the Kingdom's coming and the King's invitation to repent and enter, and equally that the message will go to *all nations*.

The seventy is both the representative number of all Israel and the representative number of all Gentile nations. Israel is both the representative of all God's people who are God's one nation, and the representative of all the nations (who will one day *all* be part of God's one people).

One further confirmation of the nature of Israel's function as representative of all is in Paul's summary account of Israel's history leading to the coming of God's promised Messiah. He states: "Then [God] destroyed seven nations in Canaan and gave their land to Israel as an inheritance" (Acts 13:19). While perfectly historical, the number seven also functions as a symbol. Throughout Scripture, it is used as the number of fullness or completion (the seven days of creation, the seven spirits of God, Jesus' "seventy times seven" of forgiveness). Here, it functions as the condensed form of the seventy Gentile nations (seven times ten). This historical reality—that seven nations inhabited the land given to Israel as an inheritance—foreshadows the reality that the fullness of God's people (comprised of every nation) will inherit the whole world. This is why Paul writes, "God's promise [was] to give the whole earth to Abraham and his descendants…" (Romans 4:13).

I am highlighting all this to underline as heavily as I am able—because I believe God in Scripture has done so—that *Israel represents all nations*. Thus, when God described to Moses exactly how the garments of the high priest were to be made, the details were incredibly significant. Here are some of those details that reveal *our assignment for prayer*.

Over the robe worn by the high priest, he was to place a linen ephod and a chest piece. God, himself, gave Moses the following instructions:

> "The craftsmen must make the ephod of finely woven linen…Take two onyx stones and engrave on them the names of the tribes of Israel. Six names will be on each stone, arranged in the order of the births of the original sons of Israel…Fasten the two stones on the shoulder-pieces of the ephod as a reminder that Aaron represents the people of Israel. Aaron will carry these names on his shoulders whenever he goes before the Lord…Then, with great skill and care, make a chest piece to be worn for making a decision from God… Mount four rows of gemstones on it…Each stone will represent one of the twelve tribes of Israel, and the name of that tribe will be engraved on it like a seal…

> In this way, Aaron will carry the names of the tribes of Israel on the sacred chest piece over his heart when goes into the Holy Place. This will be a continual reminder that he represents the people when he comes before the Lord."
>
> Exodus 28:6–29 (selected)

There is one other highly significant detail that I want to save for the end of this vision for prayer—as God has so carefully revealed it. First, think of the implications of these two garments to be worn *always whenever* the high priest enters the Holy Place. The Holy Place is where the high priest comes daily to represent the people before God. It is the place of prayer.

In the details of these garments, God is *commanding* us—as we are in fact the body of the High Priest, Jesus, on earth—to carry the names of all Israel on our shoulders, and on our hearts. What do these two carrying places signify?

The famous passage in Isaiah describing Jesus Christ states: "For a child is born to us, a son is given to us. *The government will rest on his shoulders*" (Isaiah 9:6, my emphasis).

Because Israel represents all nations, Jesus' authority over all nations is pictured in the two engraved onyx stones. In prayer as High Priest, he uses (and so *we* use) that authority to lift up and ask for the merciful, undeserved, salvation of God—now won by his own blood—for all nations.

Yes, Israel has disobeyed. Yes, every nation has disobeyed. But here is God's word: "For God has imprisoned everyone in disobedience *so he could have mercy on everyone*" (Romans 11:32). Whether it is your rebellious daughter or our governmental leaders, whether it is our neighbor or our schools, whether it is an unsaved parent or a city in turmoil—we are meant to carry them before God's great throne of grace to receive his mercy!

We are *representing* all people in prayer before God, and we ourselves *are* those stones. What that signifies is that we now stand (already) in the authority of the always increasing government of Jesus in the earth. ("There will be no end *to the increase* of his government" Isaiah 9:7, NASB, my emphasis). It is in and with that consummate authority that we pray.

And because Israel represents all nations, we can be sure that we are meant to carry all nations, and every individual person in them, before God for his merciful intervention in their lives. That each tribe—and so each nation—is engraved upon a precious gemstone pictures the much later revelation in Ephesians that each of us (and all nations) are God's "rich and glorious inheritance" (Ephesians 1:18). God, himself, is asking us to carry his own inheritance before him in prayer, to ask for them, wrestling for each and all with the widow's persistence. This is our High Priestly call.

There is this final detail as God designed these signpost garments:

> "Insert the Urim and Thummim into the chest piece so that will be carried over Aaron's heart when he goes into the Lord's presence. In this way, Aaron will always carry over his heart the objects used to determine the Lord's will for his people whenever he goes in before the Lord."
>
> Exodus 28:30

What is the significance of this final detail?

The Urim and Thummim were used when God's people needed to know what course of action God wanted them to take. When they did not know God's will, they were meant to come to the House of God to ask for his will. And in the Urim and Thummim, God would reveal his will.

Just what they were and how they functioned, no one now knows. What they represented, foreshadowed, and pointed to, however, is clear to all. They represent the coming function of the Holy Spirit. Effective prayer is not simply speaking. It is also listening for the Holy Spirit to share with us in various ways what the will of God is for the things we are praying about. And we are expectantly praying for God's decision and decisive intervention as the result of our prayers.

In prayer, we stand before God's throne—the place where decisions are rendered. The picture God is giving us in the clothing of the High Priest reinforces the authority he is placing on us to ask him to render a decision in the present, personal partnership of his Holy Spirit.

How significant are our prayers?

I hope that what I have shared in this book has deepened your understanding of the incredible weight God places on our prayers—that he acts *at our invitation*. We are his House of Prayer, his Israel wrestlers, his High Priest united in Christ Jesus.

Many years ago when America was still in its early formation, a Quaker by the name of John Woolman responded to God's call to share the Good News of Jesus' death, burial, and resurrection granting us access into the eternal Kingdom of God. A successful farmer and businessman, he used his own money to travel throughout the Northeast colonies and into regions inhabited by Native Americans sharing this message, often at the risk of his own life.

He contracted a terrible illness and lost all hope of recovery. But in the extremity of his weakness he had an experience which has impacted the lives of many people since. It is God's revelation of the importance of our prayers:

> "Although I was being carefully taken care of, my sickness was at times so intense that I lost all hope of recovery. One night in particular my suffering was great; my feet grew cold, and the cold crept up my legs toward my body. I didn't ask the nurse to apply anything warm to my feet, expecting my end to be near. After nearly ten hours in that condition, I closed my eyes thinking that at any moment I would slip out of my body. But in that instant I had a vision of the church in the earth. I felt my heart gripped with a passionate desire to see all people experience the power and blessing of God's great salvation. There was a living spring of pure love opened up in me that made me long to remain in my body, to fill up that which still is lacking in the full measure of the suffering of Christ, and to work for the good of the church.
>
> After experiencing this with such force, I asked my nurse to help warm my feet. As she did, I revived.
>
> The next evening, a good friend was visiting. I asked him to write down my experience as I described it to him, which he did as follows—'Fourth day of the first month, 1770, about five in the morning—I have seen in the Light of the Lord that the day is approaching when the man that is most wise in human policy

shall be the greatest fool; and the arm that is mighty to support injustice shall be broken to pieces. The enemies of righteousness shall make a terrible rattle, and shall powerfully torment one another. For He that is omnipotent is rising up to judgment, and will plead the cause of the oppressed. He has commanded me to reveal this vision.'

But that was not the end of God's revelation. About a week later, I experienced another vision. This time, I sent for a neighbor to come and write it down for me—because I was still too weak myself. He wrote as follows at my dictation—'The place of prayer is a precious place to dwell. What I saw was that the prayers of God's people are very precious incense. And I was given a trumpet so that I could sound forth this picture of what is true and real so that every child of God could hear it and be invited together to this precious place where the prayers of God's people, as sweet incense, rise before the very throne of God and the Lamb. I saw this place of dwelling to be safe, to be a place where there was great inner peace in the midst of tremendous upheaval and commotion in the world. Prayer, at this day, in pure, humble submission, is a precious place: the trumpet has sounded; the call goes out to the church that she gather to the place of prayer. In that place, she is forever safe.'"

John Woolman's Journal, pp. 185–186,
my updated language

"The end of the world is coming soon. Therefore, be earnest and disciplined in your prayers" (1 Peter 4:7).

Do not be deceived, dismayed, or discouraged by the power of the world and its ways. Its end is in sight! Pray earnestly and with discipline—doing it regularly, whether you feel like it or not. It is through the invitation of our prayers that God has chosen to establish his kingdom on the earth.

Let us pray.

Study/Discussion Guide

"My Father's house shall be called a house of prayer for all the nations."
Mark 11:15

"I pray because of what I believe the results will be, not because of what happens to me every time I pray."

CHAPTER ONE
Our Name is House of Prayer

Briefly describe your experience of prayer.

Use a word picture, write a poem, or draw a real picture of a house (you can include the yard), or a pie chart that you feel would most represent all aspects of your relationship with God—worship, service, giving, church, prayer, study, outreach, etc. If you are meeting with a group later, share your pictures and writings.

Had you ever thought of your life as a House of Prayer?

How does it make you feel?

Are you content with the portion that prayer represents in your word or picture drawing?

If you are, great! Take time to share with others in your group your experience of prayer with the group. If you are not satisfied (be honest), what do you like least about praying? Share with the group.

Think of some reasons why God doesn't make prayer a spiritual high each and every time you engage with Him.

What do you consider a good reason to pray?

Are there attitudes you need to change to embrace growing in your conversations with God?

PRAYER ACTION STEP

ON YOUR OWN . . .

Take time to say a prayer similar to this one. (It might be helpful to write it down and date it. You could even place a copy in your Bible).

"Lord this is where I am today. (Fill in the blank and include your current unhelpful attitudes). And I see it is not what you desire for me. I know what you want to do in me and what you even promise to do in me! Even though I don't feel like I want it, I am willing. Would you empower my heart to change and to become a more effective partner in order to help bring Your Kingdom to the world around me. I want to be included with those about whom you boast saying, 'They are my House of Prayer'".

"The faith Jesus described is faith in a Person, not a force.

***True faith that moves mountains or withers
a fig tree is Person-al faith."***

POWER TO PRAY

Study/Discussion Guide

"The earnest prayer of a righteous person has great power and produces wonderful results." James 5:16b.

"To minister in prayer simply means to serve God by praying."

CHAPTER TWO
When Shall I Pray?

Don emphasizes that there is a difference between the "Ministry <u>OF</u> Prayer" and "Ministry <u>IN</u> Prayer". In your own words describe the difference.

Does this difference help you gain perspective on your own life of prayer? Why or why not?

What four things do we learn by serving God in prayer? (Pg. 19, Paragraph 6)

    1.

    2.

    3.

    4.

Which of these things is a current growing edge for you?

Had you considered prayer a tool of learning in your growth process?

"Partnership learning can happen because when we are praying, we are disciplining ourselves to focus on God."

List the three *"When to Pray"* times.

    1.

(Mark 9: 14-29 and John 11:41-42)

    2.

(James 4:2 and James 5:13)

    3.

(Ephesians. 6:18)

Which one of these three "When to Pray" times do you find easiest?

Why?

Which is most challenging for you?

Why?

"But Lord, I thought your power is available to anyone who asks at any time."

And He answers "Yes, it is, but there is some- thing larger I am working on. It is an eternal partnership with my people."

Read Acts 19:13-16
In context with this chapter on *"When to Pray"* consider and discuss what may be some reasons the demon replied to the sons of Sceva; *"I know Jesus and I know Paul, but who are you?"*

Read Acts 4:13
How might this passage apply to your life today?

REFLECTION QUESTION:
What power do we lack because we don't pray at all times—before, during and after?

Do you believe God is ready to partner with you through prayer to see His love and purposes released in impossible situations? If not, why?

PRAYER ACTION STEP

ON YOUR OWN . . .

As you consider your life right now, is there a "kairos (decisive, God-appointed) moment" you might pray through?

Take time to pray right now.

If not, and your next kairos moment is ahead, what attitudes or adjustments in your life might you commit to God now—believing that when a "kairos moment" arrives you will handle it differently?

Make that your prayer action step.

"I have found it surprisingly against the grain to pray about that need immediately."

Study/Discussion Guide

"The greatest weariness comes from work not done." Eric Hoffer

"...here is the truth about what we are doing when we pray: we are laboring the kind of labor that is striving.

Simply put, prayer is work—hard work."

CHAPTER THREE
Prayer is Work!

Do you find viewing "prayer as work" helpful?
Why or why not?

Read I Tim.2:1-8. According to Paul how important is prayer to both the quality of life and the salvation of all people?

Discuss or write your thoughts about the relationship of prayer and salvation, and why it might be something targeted by the enemy—or so against our natural desires.

Paul writes "I have been chosen as a preacher and apostle to teach the Gentiles this message about faith and truth…". (verse7)

What connections do you see between faith, truth and prayer?

In this chapter Don talks about the transformation of the disciples' lives. They were disciples who lived with and observed close up how Jesus lived and operated out of prayer.

Before his death the disciples don't pray much; yet their lives were transformed into devotion to prayer after His death and resurrection. Don makes this observation: that their lives were transformed into pray-ers as they became disciples who took responsibility for bringing God's Kingdom on their own shoulders.

Read Mark 16:15-20. As a disciple of Jesus reflect on how you view the bringing of God's kingdom. Is it more as an observer of who God is and how he does His job, or do you take the responsibility of bringing the Kingdom in the earth as your own job description?

How might this view affect your devotion to prayer?

Why do you think it affected the prayer life of the disciples?

How have you approached prayer . . .
. . . as a skill you can learn?
. . . or as something you must be naturally good at?

Share two things you find encouraging about prayer being a skill you can learn.

    1.

    2.

"The work of prayer requires learning the skills of prayer – and anyone can learn them and keep learning them better, even me."

"As a marathoner I can learn to pray with steadiness and 'relaxed determination' knowing I can wait for prayer to unfold as I (or we together) do the work of praying."

Pg. 33

Imagine you are a Webster Dictionary. Write your definitions of:
"relaxed determination"

"prayer unfolding"

Using the 10,000-Hour Rule as a guide (Malcolm Gladwell's book, "Outliers—The Story of Success," which says it takes 10,000 hours of practice to become really, really good at something), where would you place yourself on an "established expert" scale as a pray-er?
Do you find this encouraging or discouraging?

Why?

"I need to view prayer not as a sprint but a marathon."

PRAYER ACTION STEP

ON YOUR OWN . . .
Growing in prayer is a process that happens over a lifetime.

What adjustments would you need to make to prioritize your schedule to make more time to grow your life of prayer?

Take time to commit these to God and ask for his help to follow through.

Most successful changes in life are done in small steps rather than huge leaps.

Feel free to commit these things on paper.

POWER TO PRAY

Study/Discussion Guide

"You would not have called to me unless I had been calling to you, said the Lion." C.S. Lewis, The Silver Chair

I'm not sure we've given much thought to the difficulty God faced, and still faces.

Very simply love cannot be forced, it can only be offered.

CHAPTER FOUR
Why Prayer?

Quoting Don ...
"We often confuse God's sovereignty (his ultimate authority over all things) with his rule (the active exercise of his authority)".
Pg. 74

Describe in your own words the difference between God's sovereignty and His rule.

According to Psalm 2:6-12 and Psalm 115:16, in whose authority does the "rulership" of the earth rest?

What implication does "your bearing authority on earth" have on your prayer?

Do you agree or disagree with this statement:
" ... what this means is that without our prayer God will not act, God must be invited to bring his rule because we want it."

I agree because ...

I disagree because ...

Answering as honestly as possible, on a scale of 1 to 10 (if 1 is never and 10 is in all things), where would you place your own desire to see "God's will be done on earth as it is in heaven"? How would it change your life if His will always dictated your actions?

How do you think this might affect your commitment and passion to pray?

Jesus was made a man—so he could ask God as a man—for things on behalf of man. As a man he also invited God's mercy, presence and purpose for all mankind. Does this help you to feel able to connect to the ways he prayed? Why or why not?

In this short chapter, "WHY PRAYER?" what most impacted you, and in what ways?

PRAYER ACTION STEP

ON YOUR OWN...

Write out the Lord's Prayer. Personalize and expand it. As you write this, hold this picture in your mind... you and Jesus are praying this together.

Power to Pray

Study/Discussion Guide

"Everyone who acknowledges me publicly here on earth, I will also acknowledge before my Father in heaven." Matthew 10:32

It is not that all prayers must be public, it is that some prayer should be public.

This is not just our simple idea, it is God's directive."

CHAPTER FIVE
Where Should We Pray?

In what religions other than Christianity do people pray publicly?

Why do you think they pray in public?

How do we know what Jesus prayed?

Do you agree or disagree that public prayer is something that all disciples of Jesus are commissioned by God to participate in?

Why or why not?

Have you ever prayed out loud in a public place?

If yes, was the experience challenging or easy?

Why?

When you pray in public out loud, what attitudes do you feel are helpful to hold in the front of your mind?

Thinking of prayer as conversation with a person (God), read Luke 10:13–22. How would you describe the pattern of Jesus' conversation and prayer?

For further study of Jesus' pattern of public prayer look up the following Scripture verses:
John 11:32-44   Matt. 19:13-15
John 12:23-32   Matt. 27:45-50

PRAYER ACTION STEP

ON YOUR OWN...

Make plans with a friend or friends to go into a public place and pray... OR... purpose to look for a person who is unfamiliar to you who seems to need a touch from God. Offer to pray for them on the spot.

Note: The day I did this chapter I got a call from my sister. She lives in another state and was facing a medical procedure, which had her frightened, in tears, and dreading the pain that was to come. As she sat in the waiting room unable to stop crying, a middle-aged woman approached her and said: " I don't know what is wrong, but would you mind if I prayed for you?" My sister replied; "PLEASE DO". There in the waiting room, surrounded by onlookers, the woman prayed. My sister was filled with God's peace and was able to stop crying. She went into the examining room – still feeling God's peace. After a preliminary test it was determined the painful procedure wasn't needed. My sister believes it was due to that woman's prayer and the grace of God.

Study/Discussion Guide

"For the Lord is a faithful God. Blessed are those who wait for his help."
Isaiah 30:18b

CHAPTER SIX
Our Prayer and the Helper

Think of this chapter with this subtitle, PARTNERING WITH THE HOLY SPIRIT IN PRAYER. Don and I have been "partners" for 44 years (2012), and we are pretty good at it. In fact we were chosen, along with several other couples, to play *The Newlywed Game* at a wedding party a couple of years ago. Each partner answers a series of questions while the other is out of the room. When the missing partner returns they have to guess how their mate would have answered the questions. We freaked out many people. Not only did we get all the answers correct, we used the exact same terminology to answer many of the questions. Why share this story here? It reminds me of what it's like to pray. We are here and God is in the other room . . . and somehow we need to know what to pray so he can answer. The Holy Spirit, who lives inside us, is the someone who knows his heart. However it's not so easy to catch what he is sometimes saying. In spite of how well Don and I "get" each other, sometimes it's like we pass each other in the dark. Like today—I told him I wanted to go exploring around the town we were visiting on vacation. He thought I meant I wanted to drive around the lake. After he had passed all the side streets in town and we were approaching another town. I said, "What I really wanted to do was poke around in the town we were visiting—drive around the neighborhoods and the country road of that town". "OHHH!" was his response as he turned the car around.

Communication that hits the mark is not so easy. Prayer is communication. It's an art not a science and it requires plenty of trial and error. I hope you find that encouraging. It is what this chapter is all about.

Define the word messenger.

Look up John 15:26, John 16: 7-8, 13-14. Whose messenger is the Holy Spirit?

Whose messenger are we called to be?

"One of the practical results of receiving the Holy Spirit is that he becomes a supernatural partner with each of us in praying."

List some ways that our being God's messenger might relate to prayer.

Read Ephesians 6:10-20, and respond to the following questions.

Whom are we fighting?

Where do these powers exist?

Why might it be important to stay alert?

What types of weapons are required for our battle?

Are any of the weapons or pieces of armor things you can see with your eyes or feel with your hands?

What place does God's word play in partnering with the Spirit of God?

What percentage of our prayers is to be in partnership with the Holy Spirit?

What is God concerned that we pray about?

What does the success of Paul's message depend upon?

What does this imply about how partnering in prayer with the Holy Spirit affects the work of evangelism?

PARTNERING WITH THE HOLY SPIRIT

Here are three practical steps that will help you as you partner with the Holy Spirit in prayer. Make comments on what you find helpful or not helpful about each one.

Start praying.

Listen for a voice behind you saying this is the right focus, (The Butterfly Anointing - Jack Hayford).

Pray according to the revelation you are given.

What is your experience of hearing the Holy Spirit as you pray?

Do you expect to hear his voice?

Instead of seeing revelation as the goal, we must see it as what it really is—the Coach sending in the play.

How does hearing God's voice (getting impressions)—or not hearing His voice affect your prayers?

Have you had a memorable experience of feeling like your life's schedule was interrupted to ask you to pray for something or someone? Share that experience with others in your group.

How did you know it was God who was asking you to pray?

PRAYER ACTION STEP

ON YOUR OWN...

Plan to spend 30 minutes on this exercise.

Find a quiet place where you can be alone. Quiet your heart and allow the Holy Spirit to direct whom to pray for. You will know who to apply the passage to because as you read the passage in your heart it will fit like a puzzle piece to its subject. Try praying out loud in a normal voice like you are having a conversation with God.

Look up Isaiah 30 and read through it so it becomes familiar. Then re-read it and listen for the voice of the Holy Spirit and allow him to direct your prayer as if the passage were one piece of a puzzle that fit perfectly into one of the four puzzle pieces mentioned below. Let your heart rest on only one of the subjects, disregarding the other three. Don't feel you need to pray the entire chapter not all of it will fit, just choose the portions that stand out to you). Don't be afraid to employ Jack Hayford's "Butterfly Anointing".

For your personal life... **OR**
For the life of the Church of Jesus... **OR**
For the life of someone you love... **OR**
For the life of your nation.

Study/Discussion Guide

The earnest prayer of a righteous man produces wonderful results. James 5:16

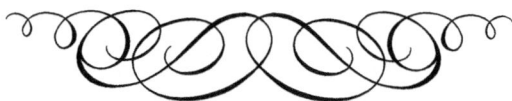

"<u>Ministry</u> engages <u>people</u> on God's behalf.
<u>Prayer</u> engages <u>God</u> on behalf of people."

CHAPTER SEVEN
The Rule of Wrestling

Describe what you believe distinguishes "earnest" prayer from "ineffective" prayer?

Read Mark 9:14-29. From this story and Jesus' final comment to his disciples (v.29), what rule or principle you could write about prayer?

What can we do to increase God's presence, power and authority in our lives?

Illustrate below, using a mathematical equation, the principle of prayer found in James 5:16b.

Mark on the scale below the spirit of your own prayers (aiming for an average).
Passionless 1 2 3 4 5 6 7 8 9 10 Earnest

What themes are you are most likely to pray earnestly for?

Re-write in your own words Habakkuk 2:4 NLT

What does it mean to live by faithfulness to God? Romans 1:17

Do you live as though your life with God is made right by faith alone?

Why do you need faith in your own heart to stand before God and pray?

Do you think of prayer as entering into a wrestling match with God?

How might this change your expectations regarding prayer?

"God <u>reveals</u> so that we may know <u>how to live a life of faith</u>."

"The secret things belong to the Lord our God, but the things revealed belong to us and to our sons forever…"
Deut. 29:29

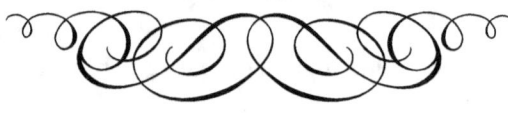

THE LAW OF WRESTLING

1. *Wrestling for God's*

    Presence All effective pray-ers have come to realize that any blessing without His presence is empty. They have come to realize that in prayer we are wrestling not for a blessing of God but for the God who brings blessings. We need him to come with it. Every request that is of God is for God." Pg.109

Try honestly to think about your prayers for God's intervention. Is getting more of God's presence what motivates your prayers?

"What it means to live a life of faith is to discover what God has revealed about himself and then live our lives as if that were in fact true."

When you've made His Presence the chief goal of your prayer, how has it influenced your prayer?

Share a challenging experience where you sought God's presence and it became the door of blessing in your situation?

> 2. Wrestling
>
> *With Who God is To wrestle effectively in prayer also means to wrestle with God—that is to wrestle with who God is. Pg.109*

Read Hebrews 4:16. According to this passage what action must we take to encounter God in prayer?

How might our imagination play a helpful role in effectively doing this?

The point is that wrestling in prayer is to argue with God for an outcome based on his character and his revealed will and promises. God is looking for active partners not passive watchers.

Do you find it easy, helpful or difficult to visualize yourself before God when you pray?

Why?

Does the idea of arguing with God make you uncomfortable or seem disrespectful?

Does a God who invites you to dialogue/argue about how he should act, change most of your view of prayer—your view of God, or your view of yourself?

Explain:

Look up Acts 9:36-42. As you read this story use your imagination to put yourself in the story.

Based on what is said to Peter (if you had been there as a silent observer) when Peter knelt down to pray, write what his prayer might have sounded like. Be sure to take time to share your version of his prayer with one another.

Read Exodus 32:1-14. Share your reflections of this passage with your group.

Do you believe your prayers can change God's mind?

> 3. *Wrestling With God Through fasting*
>
> *"... fasting is not some seldom-mentioned reserved–for–only–spiritual–giants kind of activity. It is presented in both the Old and New Testaments as a normal part of wrestling in prayer." Pg.113*

Read Deuteronomy 8:3.
What two things was God aiming for when he required people to fast?

1.

2.

Why might these things still be important for us today?

Do you find fasting a helpful tool for humbling yourself and creating dependency on God alone?

Why or why not?

> 4. *Wrestling with God Requires Persisting in Prayer.*
>
> *"I will not let you go unless me bless me." Genesis 32:26 "An inheritance gained hurriedly at the beginning will not be blessed in the end." Proverbs 20:21*

Who is God's inheritance?

How long will he wrestle for it?

Who is our inheritance?

Try to think of some reasons why we should do less wrestling than God?

What are two points Don makes about the need to be persistent in our prayers?

Pp. 115 -117

    1.

    2.

Do you find it easy or hard to persist in unanswered prayer?

Why?

PRAYER ACTION STEP

ON YOUR OWN . . .

Done on your own—unless you have a medical condition that prevents you from doing so—plan a 24 hour fast this week.

The Jewish way of fasting is from sunset of one day to sunset of the next. That means beginning your fast with dinner on one day and ending it by eating dinner the next day. You may find this method helpful. Increasing your water intake is helpful so that you don't become dehydrated.

Here are some spiritual exercises to choose from during your fast if you cannot come up with one of your own.

TAKE A PRAYER WALK
WRITE A LETTER TO GOD
PRAY THROUGH PSALM 37

POWER TO PRAY

Study/Discussion Guide

"He is seated on the throne in anticipation of our appearance."
Don Andreson

"Prayer ... is God's
arrangement for safe power sharing with us in his
intention to bless the world through us."

Dallas Willard

CHAPTER EIGHT
The Throne and The Lamb

Begin by sharing a story of when your prayer seemingly changed an outcome.

Read Hebrews 14:16. What words might you use in place of "coming boldly" and "throne of grace"?

Why, when praying, do we spiritually stand before God's throne?

Rewrite in your own words: Colossians 3:1-3

Philippians 1:27

Ephesians 2:6

What is the one and only thing that qualifies a person to stand before God and pray?

Read Revelation 5:8. Picture the scene! Where are our prayers stored and what are they doing?

When might be the only time they leave the throne room?

As you consider how long your prayers may remain with God, in what manner would you like the voice of your prayer to continue to cry out to him?

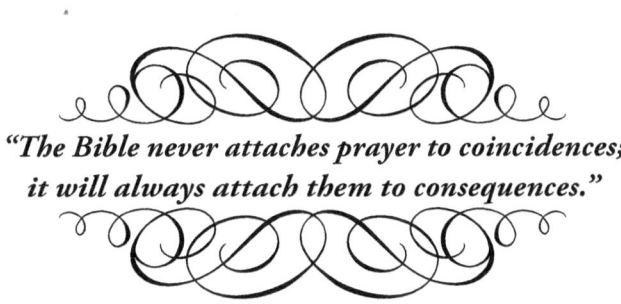

"The Bible never attaches prayer to coincidences; it will always attach them to consequences."

HOW DO WE PRAY "IN JESUS NAME"?

"I tell you the truth, anyone who believes in me will do the same works I have done, and even greater works, because I am going to be with the Father. You can ask for anything in my name, and I will do it, so that the Son can bring glory to the Father. Yes, ask me for anything in my name, and I will do it!" John 14:12-14

1. ***We pray "In Jesus' Name" when we pray things that glorify the name of Jesus. He will then in turn be free and delighted to glorify the Father by answering our prayer.***

"Our task is to pray for things that will increase and extend the honor of his name; the power sharing of God will always have this purpose." (Pg. 125) What percentage of your prayers has this as their goal?

If you began to intentionally have this as a goal, how would it change the way you pray?

"By living lives and praying prayers continually aimed at bringing glory to the name of Jesus Christ, we will be continually increasing in our boldness and authority in every prayer".

2. We pray "In Jesus' Name" when we pray according to the revealed meaning of Jesus' name.

Review Matthew 1:20-23. What did the angel of God say were the two revealed meanings of the name Jesus. (Remember that to God, a name reveals function and destiny).

What is the body and aim of prayers that reveal the name of Jesus as God with us?

Do you find yourself consistently praying for things that relate to these two desires of God's heart?

Read John 15:26 through John 16:15 In this passage Jesus identifies the name and job description of the Holy Spirit. Remember to God names reveal function and destiny. List the specifics of his job description.

The Greek word for the Holy Spirit in John 15:26 is Paraclete.

It holds within it the meanings Advocate, Helper, Comforter, Encourager, Counselor.

What other passages can you think of that describe the work of the Holy Spirit?

When you think about Jesus leaving earth so that he could send us the Holy Spirit to live within us always, (he is as present now as Jesus was present when he lived on earth in the flesh) how do you feel?

> 3. *We pray "In Jesus' Name" when we pray for God's purposes to be fulfilled according to the heart of Jesus. His heart and actions proclaim that mercy triumphs over judgment.*

Do you find it easier to pray for mercy or for judgment?

Why?

What are particular issues that offend you to the point of a self- awareness—where it is almost impossible for you to have God's heart of mercy?

Why?

Does it relate to a specific hurt you have experienced where you may need to do further forgiving?

Revelation 5:9-10

"*And they sang a new song with these words, 'You are worthy to take the scroll and break its seals and open it. For you were slaughtered, and your blood has ransomed people for God from every tribe and language and people and nation. And you have caused them to become a kingdom of priests for our God. And they will reign on the earth.'*"

According to Revelation 5:9-10, what two things does Jesus do that reveal his heart for man?

What does this say about Jesus' relationship to God the Father?

What would you say is Jesus' gift to His Father?

Chapter 1 of *Power to Pray* is titled, "Our Name is House of Prayer". It began with the story of Jesus overturning the tables of money changers and driving them from the temple—proclaiming "My Father's house shall be called a House of Prayer for all the Nations" (Mark 11:15). In this act he reveals our name and our destiny.

In Chapter 8 titled, "The Rule of Wrestling", we reviewed Jesus pre-incarnate encounter with Jacob. Here Jacob wrestles with Jesus for a blessing. Jesus blesses him by giving him a new name—Israel—"because you wrestled with God and man and won." The blessing Jesus gives is an ongoing job. We saw that Israel has a two-fold meaning—God wrestles in man and Israel wrestles with God for a blessing.

Gen. 32:22-28.

In this current chapter titled, "Throne Room of the Lamb" we conclude with Revelation 5:9-10. This revelation happens as we are approaching the end of time, as we know it.

Understand that God and Heaven are outside of time, and not confined to our space-time parameters. Here a new song is sung in heaven to Jesus. It declares who he is and what he has done!

When you think about the story line of these passages, what was Jesus always engaged in and what has been his forever goal for you?

Is he going to be successful?

PRAYER ACTION STEP

ON YOUR OWN . . .

Take time to review your notes on this chapter. As you think about "coming boldly before the Throne of Grace and you consider what it means to pray in the Name of Jesus, let the Holy Spirit rest on any area where you may need a heart change. God never overwhelms us with guilt— that is the work of the accuser. Rather he opens our eyes to see things in new ways and with hisown compassion he invites us to trust him as one with mercy and power to bring change.

Respond to the voice of the Holy Spirit by writing a prayer. See yourself presenting it to God in the Throne Room of the Lamb.

OR

Spend some time writing your own song or prayer of praise and worship glorifying and thanking the Lamb who was slain and who purchased with his blood a nation of priests, among whom you stand.

Study/Discussion Guide

"But God is so rich in mercy, and He loved us so much that even though we were dead because of our sins, He gave us life when He raised Christ from the dead." Ephesians 2:4

"Prayer for needs and prayer for nations are spoken of in the same breath. There simply is no distinction in the authority given." James 5:13–18

CHAPTER NINE
Authority to Pray for Nations

Describe in a few sentences your attitude and feelings when you are praying for:

1. Personal needs–

2. Nations–

SEVEN TESTS
In this chapter Don lists seven tests each of us must face in our journey as a disciple of Jesus (Pgs. 40-42). Review them in your book. Share which ones you feel you've passed through at least once. (Some may come around more than once.)

Which have been most challenging?

What fear did they unearth in you?

How did you overcome that fear?

Are you in the midst of a test now that you would like prayer for?

Take time in your group to share and pray for one another. If you aren't in a group make a time to get together with someone you trust, and have them PRAY with you.

THREE CHOICES

When considering praying for nations—nations are simply groups of people—Don says we are presented the same three options that Abraham (and others) had:

1. To stand on the side of judgment.

2. To say nothing or opt out of prayer.

3. To assume the responsibility and act in the authority that God's promise has conferred upon us and use it to pray for mercy.

As honestly as possible, which option is most attractive to you when you are facing the choice to pray for the people/nations that you don't like or don't agree with?

"I have always found mercy bears richer fruit than strict justice." Abraham Lincoln

PRAYER ACTION STEP

ON YOUR OWN . . .

Pick a nation that isn't your favorite nation. If you have a computer, take time to go online to Google news or another news site or go to www.operationworld.org. to get an idea of what is currently going on there. This will add content to your prayers.

Take some time to pray for that nation. Begin your prayer by asking God to give you His heart for this people or place.

Study/Discussion Guide

"Teach me your ways, O Lord, that I may live according to your truth! Grant me purity of heart so that I may honor you." Psalm 86:11

CHAPTER TEN
Or Are We Just Kidding Ourselves?

Have you ever unexpectedly been interrupted by an urgent sense you needed to pray for something or someone?

Share that experience and include any follow-up results to the experience.

"God is not all or nothing. His plans are not all or nothing. And our prayers are not all or nothing." (Pg. 58 Paragraph 3)

Do you agree or disagree with this statement, and if so, why?

Does this change your attitude about how you approach prayer?

INCREASING THE EFFECTIVENESS OF OUR PRAYERS BY LIVING IN HARMONY WITH THE WAYS OF GOD.

Look up and rewrite in your own words: Psalm 40:8

John 5:30

What does it mean to you "to live in harmony with the heart of God"?

On a scale of *one* to *ten*—if one is living totally out of harmony with God's heart, and ten is living your life like Jesus—totally in harmony with God's heart—where would you place your score?

"One of the major factors in the effectiveness of our prayers is the condition of our hearts."

"God detests the prayers of a person who ignores the law."
Proverbs 28:9

Is this score better, worse, or about the same as a year ago?

Why?

Do you feel your prayers are more or less effective than one year ago?

How about three years ago?

> INCREASING THE EFFECTIVENESS OF
> OUR PRAYERS BY EMBRACING
> REVELATION AS AN INVITATION TO PRAY.

" . . . our prayers from earth are instrumental in releasing heaven's power to earth. Many prayers have been received and preserved until God determines the appropriate time of their fulfillment." (Pg. 68, Paragraph 4)

"We know only too well that what we are doing is nothing more than a drop in the ocean.

But if the drop were not there the ocean would be missing something." Mother Teresa

Share with others a time when the answer to a prayer was delayed. Include what your experience was like and how it was resolved in your own heart.

Are there things you have given up praying for because you believed God was not listening or because you saw no answer?

Do you feel a new hope to begin praying for them again?

What types of things might God call us to pray for over a long period of time?

Personally:

In Nations:

PRAYER ACTION STEP

ON YOUR OWN...

Is there an area of your life that you know is out of harmony with the heart of God?

Take time to repent—giving it to God and seeking His intervention.

OR...

Begin again the process of praying for something you had put aside because you were disheartened about a delayed response.

POWER TO PRAY

Study/Discussion Guide

"Truth cannot be defeated." Edwin Louis Cole

"The words of God are words God in heaven longs to fulfill. He waits only for his partners on earth to ask."

CHAPTER ELEVEN
Praying That Works

In the first sentence of this chapter Don uses the word "tool" to describe God's word. Write down all the characteristics you can think of that describe a good tool.

When in a discussion with another, and they use your own words as evidence to make their point, how do you feel?

Children, spouses and parents are particularly gifted with the ability to remember what you once said. Why do you think this is true?

What might be some of the reasons behind the misuse of God's word in prayer?

How do you expect God to deal with prayers based on a misuse of his word?

MEMORIZE JEREMIAH 23:29

"Does not my word burn like fire?" says the Lord. Is it not like a mighty hammer that smashes a rock to pieces?"

AND . . . ISAIAH 55:10-11

"The rain and snow come down from the heavens and stay on the ground to water the earth. They cause grain to grow, producing seed for the farmer and bread for the hungry. It is the same with my word. I send it out, and it always produces fruit. It will accomplish all I want it to and will prosper everywhere I send it."

"...The word of God is truth and has the power of truth—when aimed correctly. It's not a toy gun, and it's not a fake gun."

Here are some reasons that Jesus (our model) depended upon God's Word:

1. God's Word has power because it is true. (Proverbs30:5)

2. It is God's truth revealed specifically to us— so that we might apply it to life. (Matt. 4:4, Luke 4:4, Deut.8:3)

3. It is living and powerful. (Heb.4:12, 11:3, Jeremiah 23:29, Isaiah 55:10-11)

4. It conveys the will of God. (Psalm119)

5. We live in the midst of a "spiritual" battle and God's Word is the (our) "spiritual" offensive weapon crafted and forged by God himself for our joint victory over the enemy. (Eph. 6:13- 17)

Which of the above reasons motivate you the most and why?

Rate yourself on the scale of 1 to 10 below with 1 being "I seldom pray God's Word, and 10 being "I regularly pray God's Word".

1 2 3 4 5 6 7 8 9 10

What would you commit to do to move up the scale a notch or two over the next two months?

In conclusion, what chapters from Don's book, *Power to Pray*, most changed your view of prayer?

Why?

If you are doing this book within the context of a group, take time to share your answers with one another.

Pray for one another in the areas you would each like to experience change in your prayer life.

PRAYER ACTION STEP

ON YOUR OWN...

Using Don's model of praying a passage of scripture, choose a favorite Psalm and pray it this week.

If you don't have a favorite Psalm here are some of my favorites.

Psalm 103

Psalm 91

Psalm 126

Psalm 127

Psalm 29

Psalm 1

Psalm 92

Psalm 146

Psalm 23

BIBLIOGRAPHY

Gladwell, Malcolm. Outliers—The Story of Success. London, England: Allen Lane, 2008.

Jacobs, Cindy. Possessing The Gates Of The Enemy. Grand Rapids, Michigan: Chosen Books, 1994.

Laubach, Frank. Man of Prayer. Syracuse, New York: Lauback Literacy International, 1990.

Murray, Andrew. The State of The Church. Kempton Park, South Africa: The Andrew Murray Consultation of Prayer for Revival and Missions, 1985.

O'Martian, Stormie. The Power of A Praying Nation. Eugene, Oregon: Harvest House Publishers, 2002.

Paul, Annie Murphy. New York Times Book Review. March 21, 2010.

Prince, Derek. Shaping History Through Prayer And Fasting. New Kensington, Pennsylvania: Whitaker House, 1973.

Sandford, John. Healing The Nations—A Call To Global Intercession. Grand Rapids, Michigan: Chosen Books, 2000.

Shenk, David. The Genius In All Of Us: Why Everything You've Been Told About Genetics, Talent, and IQ Is Wrong. New York: Doubleday, 2010.

Voskamp, Ann. One Thousand Gifts. Grand Rapids, Michigan: Zondervan, 2010

Willard, Dallas. Knowing Christ Today—Why We Can Trust Spiritual Knowledge. New York: Harper-Collins, 2009.

Wilson, J. Christ, Jr. More To Be Desired Than Gold. Wilson, 1992.

Wood, Alan and Jamie. <u>Third Cord Secret—Discover The Secret Of A Highly Successful Marriage</u>. Mobile, Alabama: Gazelle Press, 2009.

Woolman, John. <u>The Journal of John Woolman</u>. The John Greenleaf Whittier Text. New York: Corinth Books Inc., 1961.

ABOUT THE AUTHOR

Don Andreson is the founding pastor (along with his wife, Nancy) of The Vineyard–A Community Church in Kingston, Massachusetts, first begun in 1985. In addition to teaching in conferences and seminars, he and Nancy have led many teams devoted to prayer both internationally and locally. Don is a graduate of Princeton University (BA) and Gordon-Conwell Theological Seminary (MDiv). He and Nancy have four wonderful children and fourteen grandchildren.

www.ingramcontent.com/pod-product-compliance
Lightning Source LLC
Chambersburg PA
CBHW071430070526
44578CB00001B/60